BULLSHIFT!

MONEY DOES GROW ON TREES

BULLSHIFT!

MONEY DOES GROW ON TREES

*The No Bullsh*t Way to Rewire Your*
MONEY MINDSET
for Real Business Growth

MARLA TABAKA

Bullshift! Money Does Grow on Trees
 Published by Growth Mind Media

For more information, visit: *marlatabaka.com*

ISBN: 979-8-9942812-0-8 (Paperback) Additional ISBNs for other formats are available upon request.

 This book is for informational and educational purposes only and does not constitute professional financial, legal, therapeutic, or medical advice.

This book is for informational and educational purposes only and does not constitute professional financial, legal, therapeutic, or medical advice. The author and publisher assume no responsibility for actions taken based on the contents of this book.

The neuroscience concepts discussed in this book are intended to support awareness and personal growth and are not a substitute for professional medical or mental health care.

Growth Mind Media books are available at a discount when purchased in quantity for sales promotions or corporate use. For more information, please email *marla@marlatabaka.com*

Cover Design by Kimberly Schaefer
Interior Layout by Frank Gutbrod Design
Developmental Editing by Rosanna Harpest
Edited by Cheryle Lichtenberger
Edited by Cheryl Steele

Printed in the United States of America
First Edition

Bullshift

verb

[bool-shift]

1. to convert self-limiting beliefs into empowering thoughts, effectively neutralizing the detrimental narratives within one's mind and thereby eliminating mental barriers to unlock the doors of wealth, happiness, and success.

    I. **Synonyms:** Mindset alchemy, belief transformation, cognitive recalibration, success-minded.

    II. **Antonyms:** Stagnation, self-doubt, limiting beliefs, mindset inertia, lack-minded.

Contents

Acknowledgements

For everyone who dares to believe they are capable of more.
Your courage is the spark that changes everything.

And to the entrepreneurs who have walked this path with me.
Your willingness to be vulnerable, courageous, and open to transformation is what has truly brought the Bullshift tools to life.
Your journeys continue to inspire this work, and others, in ways words can barely capture.

Before you begin . . .

This book is not meant to be read once and set aside. It is meant to be experienced.

You may find yourself wanting to read straight through, and that's perfectly fine. But the real transformation happens when you slow down, reflect, and put the tools into practice. The exercises throughout this book are designed to help you notice old patterns, create new awareness, and gently rewire how you think, feel, and respond, especially around money, confidence, and possibility.

Because the Bullshift exercises build on one another, it's important to complete them in the order they appear. Each exercise lays the foundation for the next, even when the connection isn't immediately obvious. Trust the sequence and give yourself time with each step before moving forward.

You don't need to rush, and you don't need to get it "right." Give yourself space between chapters if something stirs emotion or insight. Growth doesn't happen on a schedule. It happens when awareness and action meet.

Most of all, be kind to yourself as you move through this work. Lasting change is built through curiosity, honesty, and practice, not pressure.

Introduction

P*oof!* Gone in an instant . . . One poor decision, and I lost $1,000,000. I had planned to retire by age 55, and I was on track to achieve that goal.

Imagine waking up one morning to face the fact that your bank account has been drained, your investments have vanished, and your financial security has been shattered. Devastating can't begin to describe the downfall and fear that shook me to the core. The truth didn't trickle in. It crashed down on me like a wave I never saw coming. I had been living in a haze of false hope that I had made the right financial decisions, but in one unbearable moment, the fog cleared, and I was staring straight into financial ruin.

Have you ever watched your hard-earned money disappear in what feels like an instant—along with your dreams, your confidence, and your sense of security? Panic takes over. Your thoughts spiral. And then the gut-punch question slams in: *Now what?*

When everything crumbles, it's easy to feel like the world is against you. The mind scrambles for answers: *Why is this happening? Who's to blame? What did I do wrong?* And that's where many of us get stuck.

Are you struggling in business or just getting by? Perhaps you haven't gotten to the point of having much money to lose? Who or what do you blame for the struggle? Is the economy so crippling that you can't pay your bills or save for the future? Did you experience a loss as I did? Are your employees "lazy" and unproductive? Do you have prospects and customers who just don't get it? Have the stars (mis)aligned to bring you one misfortune after another? If you were attracted to this book, my guess is you don't have the cash flow, savings, or spending money you'd like to have. Or perhaps you're doing okay but don't get to enjoy the luxuries you see others experiencing, like vacations, dining out, and an impressive wardrobe.

Now, 20 years of working with entrepreneurs (along with the ups and downs of my personal journey) have taught me that each of us possesses the ability to consciously change our circumstances even when it seems like the world is working against us. We are also capable of bringing more money into our lives and businesses. If you run a small business, you don't need investors or a wealthy uncle who leaves his fortune to you in his will, you need a *growth mindset* that includes undeniable faith in the power of your thoughts. The solutions to your money problems lie within you and are incredibly simple! However, that doesn't mean they're easy. That's why I created what I call the Bullshift Process: a set of tools, knowledge, and insights that have empowered my clients to release their damaging, limiting beliefs and turn their dreams into reality. And you will too!

But here's the thing—most people don't realize they're operating under a set of limiting beliefs that keep them stuck in financial struggle. It's very limiting to think that success is just about working harder, finding more clients, or cutting expenses. True success comes from shifting your mindset and rewriting the negative internal narrative that shapes your relationship with money. It's about struggling less, not more, and thinking in a way that brings opportunity, clarity, and confidence into your life.

That's where the Bullshift Process comes in. It's not magic, but it sure feels like it once you see the results. This book is designed to help you uncover the hidden blocks that keep you from reaching your financial potential and give you the tools to shift into a whole new way of thinking, one that attracts money and success instead of repelling it.

WHY I WROTE THIS BOOK AND HOW IT WORKS

Small businesses are the heartbeat of this nation, yet most fail. Some 20 years ago, when I became a business coach, I was determined to find ways to make funding more accessible to business owners. *It's unfair*, I thought, *that so many of the financial benefits offered by the government and investors go to big businesses while small businesses are basically on their own.*

I quickly learned that while access to funding is indeed problematic, it's more than just the politics of money that causes businesses to fail. The problem lies within the minds of entrepreneurs, namely their money mindset and their engrained belief that success is hard.

As a coach, I've watched in awe as my clients went from the daily grind and financial struggle to multiple six- and seven-figure revenues. I've witnessed their pain turn to joy. I've seen them grow into leaders and create opportunities for others to thrive. This transformation begins by helping my clients explore their limiting beliefs about themselves, the people in their lives, the world around them, and money. I teach my clients that it's not access to money that determines your future wealth: it's your relationship with money that does it. Only with this understanding can my clients break free from financial struggle and unlock true success. Entrepreneurs must first shift their mindset because the way you think about money ultimately shapes how much of it you attract and keep.

Every entrepreneur deserves a shot at success without a negative belief system, especially one about money, holding them back! That's why I'm excited to introduce you to the Bullshift Process.

As you read this book, you'll learn how your brain and subconscious mind work together to create your reality.

Unfortunately, if you don't have what you want in life and business, it means that much of your reality is likely based on the BS stories you tell yourself! In these pages, you'll learn to identify the false narratives your mind engages in and how they hold you back. The information and exercises here will help you identify your money story and eradicate the negative aspects that keep you from accumulating wealth and finding your way as a happy, successful entrepreneur. You'll discover insights, exercises, provocative questions, and success stories designed to help you shift away from those limiting beliefs.

Using the methodology in this book, many of my clients have turned their grim financial picture around in only a few months. You can do that, too! Some take longer, depending on how engrained their negative belief patterns are, or how limiting their mindset is. But no matter how long it takes, it's far better than remaining in your current financial state for the foreseeable future! As you move through these pages, try not to skip the exercises—or just *think* about your answers. Write them down. There is real power in seeing your thoughts on paper. It will help you:

- Spot patterns in your thoughts and behaviors.
- Make surprising connections between past experiences and current challenges.
- Unpack negative thoughts you've been avoiding or ignoring.
- Bring to light stories from your past that are quietly shaping your relationship with money.
- Build a written record you can revisit whenever you feel stuck.
- Clarify your goals and start mapping out how to reach them.

My hope and wish for you is that you will experience many aha! moments as you discover your true self and learn to plant, nurture, and grow your money tree. I've designed the path for you to Bullshift from your limiting money mindset (all those BS stories you tell yourself) to a powerful mindset of magnetism that will attract the freedom, happiness, and wealth you deserve.

MONEY DOESN'T GROW ON TREES—BULLSHIFT!

A limiting money mindset may cause you to spend (usually unwisely) what money you have or guard every cent with worry. The adage "Money doesn't grow on trees" suggests that we struggle to earn money and that it can easily slip through our fingers—so we better be careful with the money we have. While squandering your money is probably unwise (and another red flag indicating a poor money mindset), holding on too tightly could exacerbate your fear of being without it. Fear is loud and intense, so it's the signal your brain locks onto, shutting out thoughts of comfort and abundance. A fearful, limiting perspective on money will keep you from acquiring a successful business and satisfying income.

Did you know that most countries manufacture paper money from wood fibers? Trees, quite literally, give life to currency! However, here in the U.S., our dollars are a blend of 75% linen and 25% cotton—not the mighty oak or stately pine. So, no, money doesn't grow *directly* on trees, but it remains a perfect metaphor for building a thriving money mindset.

Picture your money tree rooted in rich, fertile soil. These roots represent your foundational beliefs about money and your relationship with it. If those beliefs are shallow or the soil is depleted, your tree will struggle to grow. But when the soil is well fertilized with positive beliefs and healthy habits, your tree's roots grow strong, anchoring you in abundance and opportunity.

The trunk of your money tree is your financial core, fortified by the insights and exercises in this book designed to grow and transform your money mindset. As your core becomes more resilient, it supports the far-reaching branches of your dreams: new opportunities, financial growth, and emotional well-being. Now, look up at the bright green leaves bursting from the branches. These represent your wealth, investments, and future potential. Imagine them shimmering in the sunlight, so bountiful that you can share their shade and fruit with family, friends, and causes close to your heart.

Like any tree in your backyard or favorite park, your money tree requires care and attention. From the deep roots of your beliefs to the vibrant leaves of your success, you have the power to cultivate a flourishing financial mindset. Start here, nurture your progress, and watch your money tree grow tall and strong, a symbol of your newfound abundance and fulfillment.

Imagine your money tree taking root with each idea a seed waiting to sprout into abundance. The Bullshift Process will help you do that. These practices are not just theory; they are backed by neuroscience and solid research on how small changes can lead to big results.

Now, with that nourishing thought in mind, let me share how my own transformation began—unexpected, messy, and full of surprising lessons. So, get comfortable, and let's rewind to where it all began . . .

CHAPTER 1
The Backstory . . .

At age 27, I did what many young people do: I married the man I loved. Next up, a baby. Never did I expect that we would be mysteriously blessed with twins, even though there was no history of twins on either side of the family. Having hoped for two kids, one pregnancy resulting in two children was fine with me and a welcome one. Little did I know there was a reason I was granted my wish for two children in this joyfully convenient way.

When our daughters were six months old, we moved from the city of Chicago to Naperville, Illinois, about 30 miles outside of the city. My husband and I now had a modest yet spacious home, two healthy daughters, and a loving relationship. It felt like a dream come true! And then a devastating tsunami abruptly interrupted our happy life.

Just two months after we moved to Naperville, my husband Wally visited the doctor complaining of fatigue and a persistent cough. After undergoing all the standard tests, Wally had a follow-up visit with his doctor to learn the results, which he scheduled on our second wedding anniversary. Who would schedule such a thing on his wedding anniversary? Well, that was my husband. Nothing ever seemed like a big deal to him, and he considered worry a total waste of time. I handled the worrying—and did enough of it for both of us.

When I didn't hear from Wally for hours after he was due home from his follow-up visit, my anxiety grew. Fear clenched in my gut, along with conflicting emotions of anger and loving concern. At 6:15 on that sunny evening, the phone finally rang.

I heard Wally's voice break as emotion took hold, but even that couldn't prepare me for the words I was about to hear. In an instant my mind flashed to cancer, surely we could deal with that. I would be strong for him; we would fight this together. But the C word didn't come out of his mouth. Instead, I heard, "I don't think I should come home." I couldn't relate as I stumbled in my thoughts. *What?* Why would he think such a thing?

Confused and anxious, I couldn't even imagine the enormity of what was next to come. "Of *course,* you should come home," I encouraged, trying my best to keep negative thoughts at bay. "It's our anniversary! Where are you?" Wanting to hold on to a sense of normalcy for as long as possible, I added, "You're late for dinner, honey. Please, just come home."

I was shaking; my breathing was increasingly shallow. I remember the sensation of lightheadedness as if it were yesterday and not so many years ago.

"Oh God, Marla, I have HIV!" Wally cried. Stunned beyond words, I couldn't speak or even cry. His words simply would not register. Human Immunodeficiency Virus? It was 1987, and I had only recently heard of this devastating new epidemic. Children who tested HIV-positive were banned from school; in one case, their home was burned to the ground by frightened, angry residents. President Reagan had just given his first national speech on the disease.

This was a time when a diagnosis of HIV always led to full-blown AIDS—Acquired Immune Deficiency Syndrome, a literal death sentence! It was *not possible* that now my husband had HIV and that he would die a young, painful death. My mind began reeling

. . . and then it hit me. Not only would Wally be taken from us by this highly contagious, devastating disease, but our whole precious family would soon become only a memory to those who loved us. AIDS would condemn me to watch our innocent babies die a horrid death—that is, if I didn't die first! This. Was. *Not.* Happening!

I couldn't be HIV-free since we hadn't taken precautions. No. This nightmare simply could *not* be happening. Denial and a litany of agonizing thoughts ran through my mind in only seconds, vivid images of horrific events to come. The pain was unbearable. What seemed like hours of processing took only seconds.

"Marla, what should I do?" Wally pleaded. "I don't know what to do!"

"You have to come home! Of *course* you should come home," I cried. "Please come home!"

I rushed to hang up the phone with an irrational thought running through my mind: *If I hung up quickly, this nightmare would end.* As I came to my senses, the reality of this waking nightmare racing through my mind became overwhelmingly clearer. Running into our bathroom, the only truly private space in the house, I collapsed into a fetal position face down on the cold floor. Tormented by the silent screams that couldn't escape my mouth for fear our little girls would become frightened, I instinctively covered my head with my arms. Every cell of my being hurt; my heart felt crushed under the world's weight. My babies were going to die. My husband was going to die. I wished with all my might that *I* could die right then, right there in that tiny space. It felt humanly impossible to bear this pain.

I wish I could say I was strong and quickly gathered my wits to prepare for my husband's return home, but I don't remember what happened in the next hour. I don't recall being strong; I only remember being panic-stricken with a warped belief that everything would be fine, that this shocking news was not true. I was in denial.

Upon seeing him I immediately ran into Wally's embrace in the garage as he hesitantly stepped out of the car with a bouquet of anniversary flowers in his arms. I can still smell their sickly-sweet aroma. (Please never send me carnations or those giant orange lilies!)

Wally later told me he wasn't sure I would touch him or want to be touched by him. To this day, I still can't imagine what that must have felt like.

The following seven years were the longest of my young life—and the last of Wally's. We were blessed with a clean bill of health for me, and thank God, also for our daughters. If I hadn't believed in miracles at the time, I quickly learned that miracles do indeed happen. Wally would have been infected before our marriage; the odds of me remaining free of the deadly virus were slim to none. The doctors were amazed. No words could convey the depth of gratitude and joy for the fact that our children did not come into this world with a death sentence and that I would remain on this planet to see them into adulthood.

Yet there were times when it felt nearly impossible to remain grateful for our good fortune. Remember, Wally's diagnosis was in 1987, before sharing more openly about having HIV or AIDS felt understood like today. No, we could not tell a soul. This journey was ours to travel alone, leaving us with a nearly unmanageable, dark secret that could go no further than our frightened minds. We did not even tell my parents or our siblings; the risks were too high. I knew that my father, who had tendencies toward hypochondria, would never have entered our home again had he known. My mother would have taken on the burden of our pain. Our children would have been removed from school, and Wally would have lost his job. Even friends would have disappeared for fear of catching the deadly disease, and I couldn't blame them. AIDS was in the news daily, accompanied by warnings of its contagious and deadly nature. It was a painful, lonely time, even though we had one another.

Yet another miracle occurred for us as we traversed the next seven years: The virus caused comparatively minimal effects on Wally's health. While he did eventually suffer from bouts of pneumonia and meningitis, it could have been so much worse. Even though he didn't experience a miraculous recovery, Wally remained healthy enough, allowing us to keep our secret. My husband worked right up until the day he entered the hospital for the final time. That was on Halloween; this deadly disease displayed a sick sense of humor.

The most profound and complicated part of Wally's passing was that we never got to say goodbye. We had spent over seven years dreading this unavoidable tragedy, and despite our foreknowledge, I was not able to hold my husband's hand and look into his eyes for one last time, missing the opportunity to tell him how much I loved him—or to hear those exact precious words from him. The day after the doctor admitted Wally to the hospital, they performed a lung biopsy, deciding to put him into a three or four-day medically induced coma to "heal." We had no way of knowing that three and a half weeks later, on the Friday after Thanksgiving in November of 1994, Wally would take his last natural breath. That was only one day after his pulmonologist delivered the wonderful news that Wally had taken a turn for the better and would be home to us by Christmas, he promised me.

On that sunny Friday morning, while out gift shopping for my husband and children, celebrating the doctor's promise of a homecoming by Christmas, my cell phone rang. "Mrs. Tabaka, you need to get to the hospital as quickly as possible," the nurse advised. "Something unexpected has happened, and I don't believe Mr. Tabaka will be with us much longer." My world shook . . . *What??* Had I heard her right? How much longer? Minutes, hours? She could not tell me.

Thirty minutes later, I went running through the corridors of the ICU until I saw the outstretched arms of a nurse I did not know. She was shaking her head as she stood firmly in front of the curtain that separated Wally's bed from the corridor. I knew he was gone, but there was something more behind that curtain—something she did not want me to witness.

The hours that followed my arrival at the ICU were a blur of ridiculous missteps by the hospital staff. As I waited anxiously in the corridor, the nurse couldn't figure out how to disconnect Wally's ventilator, which kept her from allowing me to approach his bed upon my arrival. My husband was breathing, yet unreachable.

Right next to me, the nurses laughed merrily as they placed their custom orders for cheeseburgers. "I'd like cheese, tomatoes, lettuce, and mayonnaise, but hold the mustard. And don't forget the fries," the nurse who was in the room with my husband shouted.

After 10 agonizing minutes of the nurses holding me at bay while repeated attempts to remove my husband's ventilator failed, I pushed through the curtain to be at his side. In the end, my final goodbye was to a dead husband who was still breathing.

The social worker they'd called to come to my aid insisted I sign a consent form to donate Wally's organs. I might have saved some lives that day when I refused to do so. You know, since my husband had AIDS and all. Then she pressed me to call someone to pick me up, but there was no one. All my friends and family were traveling for the Thanksgiving holiday. The social worker snapped, "Oh, come on, you must have someone to call!" That was the last straw. I wasn't just alone; I was completely untethered from the outside world. I was well beyond any breaking point.

How do you pop into a hospital to confirm that, yes, your loved one is dead, and then turn around and drive yourself home to your children as though nothing is out of place? The whole world was amiss—shattered.

The whole thing felt surreal, and still, what hurt most were the goodbyes left unspoken. We were robbed of those special moments for him to express his last wishes, and he never had the opportunity to tell me that everything would be all right. Oh, how I needed to hear him say that everything would be okay someday! We. Did. Not. Say. Goodbye. Not until three days after his death.

SHAPING OUR NEW REALITY

A blur of challenging and demanding events filled the days after the nightmare at the hospital. Coming home on the day Wally died, I knew I had to break many hearts with the dreadful news, like walking into a battle unarmed. How could I tell his mother that she had lost yet another son? What do you say to two 8-year-old children anticipating their father's return as the best Christmas present ever? What words would I use to support Wally's wishes and continue the lies surrounding his mysterious illness and now death? His request now felt impossible, but you know what? I believed I could do it, and so I did.

At first, my motivation was guilt. How could I deny my husband his desire for secrecy; how could I go against his wishes after nearly eight years of working so hard to keep our secrets? But then, thinking of what was best for my children, a surge of protectiveness and resolute energy came upon me, and I shifted my mindset from one of guilt to one of determination.

I told myself I was strong and capable and that I could carry this weight and live through it while supporting my children in their time of grief and loss. That 30-minute drive home closed the darkest chapter of my life and opened the door to a new journey—one where grief would give way to growth. At this moment the Bullshift Process quietly took root, signaling the birth of my growth mindset and a spiritual awakening that would change everything. I just didn't know it yet.

The things we wish for *can* become our reality if we believe in our ability to manifest them. This painful event held a hidden gift under its bleak exterior: It allowed me to choose between wallowing in thoughts of a dismal future or developing greater strength and shifting toward a new set of beliefs that would change my world.

THREE DAYS LATER

At some all-too-soon point, everyone who suffers the loss of a loved one must watch the friends, coworkers, and family who appear by their side to support them return to their own lives. When that point in time came for me, I knew that if I didn't lean on something different—a source or power greater than myself—I would not be capable of parenting my children in the way they deserved and needed. For the first time since I had long ago turned my back on an old-fashioned Catholic upbringing that made no sense to me, I asked for help from a higher power. Call it God, the Universe, Mystical Energy, or whatever you'd like. I prayed hard, cried hard, and demanded hard truths.

What should I do next? How could I go on without the support of the man I loved? How could I manage a three-hour commute, a career, and raising a family alone? And how in the world could I manage financially on only one income? "Damn it, tell me! Tell me *now*!" I demanded.

After exhausting a litany of demands, I collapsed face down, arms spread wide onto the bed I had shared with my husband for years. I cried like never before, feeling lost and desperately determined to release the unbearable pain.

Suddenly and mysteriously, the fear and pain vanished. I could not feel or access that unrelenting agony even if I tried. I felt nothing. I didn't even experience fear when I discovered that I could not move. Not my arms, not my legs, not even my head. The only sensation was one of a gentle, soothing weight that covered my entire body. My tears dried, and complete peace took the place of my intense fear and anxiety. I'd never in my whole life experienced such peace and calmness. Such a sense of comfort and security was foreign to me.

And then the most unexpected thing happened! I may not be able to put this into words that make sense to you, but I think that's because it's not supposed to make sense—it just *was*.

Planted in a single heartbeat, like a seed of knowing within me, was the complete and total acceptance of what was now an undeniable fact: Everything would be fine. I was safe and my girls were safe. We would be taken care of, and we would find happiness once again. I knew then that money would soon be no object; in fact, we would have more money, joy, and happiness than I had ever imagined could be possible under these circumstances.

The following moments were the most miraculous of my life, even more so than when I'd learned that the girls and I were HIV-free. Wally was *there*. His was the soothing weight that lifted my pain and held me in place, leaving me unable to move my limbs. He stilled me; he stilled my pain and fear. His loving voice filled the air, saying, "I love you more than you'll ever know, Mar. Everything is going to be all right. I promise you this."

Have you ever had a moment when a new thought or belief, a new awareness about something that needed to change in your life, or a novel concept for your business just hits you out of nowhere? Like suddenly, something was meant to happen, and you knew you were the one chosen to carry out the mission? This is that seed of knowing that I experienced in these moments, like a transformation of the mind that you cannot ignore.

Slowly, the mysterious weight lifted. Wally wasn't gone; I could feel him in my heart. And I knew beyond the shadow of a doubt that our little family would somehow be taken care of and that I could focus on managing my grief and helping our girls to do the same.

That moment changed everything. It did not erase my grief or remove my challenges, but it awakened something inside me. I felt a level of strength, faith, and clarity I had never known before. I did not realize it then, but that was the beginning of a journey that would reshape my life and eventually lead to the creation of the Bullshift Process.

CHAPTER 2

The Story Behind Bullshift

The experience I had that day became a turning point in my life. I did not just rebuild my world after loss; I rebuilt myself from the inside out. Over time, I discovered that when you change your thoughts, your reality begins to change as well. That realization lit a fire in me. I knew I was meant to share what I had learned with others who were silently struggling. I wanted to understand this transformation on a deeper level so I could teach it, not just live it.

That calling eventually led me into the world of coaching where, after years of working with entrepreneurs and writing for publications like Inc., Times Business, and Huffington Post, I built a powerful toolkit of mind-shifting strategies. Whether through one-on-one coaching, podcasts, or my published work, I have helped hundreds of thousands, perhaps millions, of people tackle challenges, shift their mindset, and take bold steps forward.

I had gathered and built these powerful mind-shifting tools, but I could not find a name that captured the essence of this work. It was incredibly frustrating because I knew how life-changing these strategies were, yet I did not know how to package them in a way that people would immediately understand. In my coaching practice, I watched people break lifelong patterns, increase their income, heal anxiety, rebuild confidence, and step into lives they once believed were out of reach. I knew something powerful was happening and I needed to document it and share it with the world.

I wanted a simple term that would speak to entrepreneurs and reflect the impact of this transformation in just one or two words. I needed something memorable that would draw people in and help them recognize the value of this work.

Then finally, Bullshift was born.

Brilliance can be born in an instant and dinner with Christie Ruffino, a fellow coach and good friend, offered just that opportunity. Christie has helped hundreds of fellow authors bring their stories to the public through speaking and publishing. As I vented about my "block," Christie turned my complaining into a coachable moment. "Marla?" she asked, "What is it that really pisses you off?"

It did not take a second for the answer to form. I already knew exactly what I needed to say. "What really pisses me off," I replied, "is the number of brilliant entrepreneurs out there who tell themselves bullshit lies about their ability to succeed. They don't believe in themselves or the world around them. All of this BS only holds them back. If only they could get out of their own damn way! They just need to shift their thinking to a healthy, productive mindset that gets them what they want and deserve; they just don't know it yet!"

In that moment, something clicked. Christie looked at me with quiet certainty and said one powerful, made-up word: "Bullshift." We both went silent as the word settled between us. It instantly captured the essence of my work and the transformation I had been guiding people through for years! When the silence finally broke, we both knew it. We could feel the power of it instantly. Bullshift was born.

From that moment, everything changed. I developed my Bullshift Group Coaching series and began documenting the Bullshift Process so I could teach it to others. That work eventually led to the writing of this book. Since a lack of money is one of the most significant challenges entrepreneurs face, I decided to focus the Bullshift tools in this book on the money mindset.

Your money mindset is your internal script about money. It reflects what you believe you deserve, how you handle money, and whether you attract it or push it away. For entrepreneurs, it can be the difference between barely getting by and building lasting wealth.

And here we are, you and me, connected through a shared desire for more. More clarity. More confidence. More financial freedom. You might be meeting me for the first time, but I know your world well. The stakes are high in entrepreneurship; money can show up fast and disappear just as quickly. That rise-and-fall pattern has crushed businesses and dreams more times than we can count.

It almost crushed mine once.

I know what it feels like to work hard, to care deeply, and still feel like something invisible is holding you back. I know what it is like to question yourself, to wonder if you are missing something everyone else has figured out. I know how heavy it feels when your potential does not match your results. If that sounds familiar, you are not alone.

THE REAL STRUGGLE

What I once believed was a personal flaw turned out to be a universal block, especially for entrepreneurs. Some get stuck in the exhausting win and lose cycle. Others never make enough money to lose in the first place. It may look like a revenue problem, a sales problem, or a strategy problem, but it is not. The real problem lives in your brain. It is the unexamined beliefs, unchallenged fears, and subconscious patterns that quietly run your life and your business without your permission.

This is why so many smart, talented, hardworking people stay stuck. They chase productivity hacks, new marketing tactics, and business courses that promise success, yet nothing changes long term. Why? Because mindset always overrides mechanics. You will never outperform your beliefs about what you deserve. Until you upgrade your internal operating system, you will keep recreating the same financial reality over and over again.

We have been taught to believe that making money is a struggle and that only a lucky few truly succeed. But what if everything you were taught about money is wrong? *Bullshift! Money Does Grow on Trees* debunks the myths holding you back and teaches you how to cultivate lasting wealth from the inside out. I have been where you are, facing setbacks and uncertainty. I found my way out by rewiring my mindset, clearing emotional resistance, and creating a new relationship with money. You can do the same. In fact, you are about to.

ENTREPRENEURSHIP: THE WORLD'S CRAZIEST ROLLERCOASTER RIDE

Yup, I'd like to welcome you to the wildest rollercoaster in the world: Entrepreneurship: where fortunes are made only to be lost in the blink of an eye. There are twists and turns, ups and downs, and sometimes the force of the ride leaves you spiraling. You might want to get off this crazy roller coaster, but something keeps you going, something that others may not understand. This challenging cycle breaks businesses, and dreams, every single day.

Some adventurers conquer the ride and enjoy the thrill. Some entrepreneurs get stuck in the win-or-lose cycle, while others never make enough money to lose in the first place. It almost doesn't matter whether you're riding high or hanging on through a downturn. In both cases, your mindset is what drives the ride.

No matter where you are on the ride, one thing is clear. What you believe about money will shape how you experience it.

But to change the way you think about money, you first need to understand what shapes your thoughts in the first place. That means we need to take a closer look at the most powerful tool you have for transformation: your brain.

CHAPTER 3
Meet Your Brilliant Brain

Most people try to change their money habits by focusing on external fixes like budgeting apps, hustle strategies, or spreadsheets. But lasting change doesn't begin in your wallet. It begins in your brain. You don't need a neuroscience degree to rewire your money mindset, just a basic understanding of a few essential brain functions can make the journey of changing your beliefs faster and smoother. By understanding how your brain quietly shapes your habits and emotions, you'll gain practical tools to create transformation, starting right now by taking a tour of your subconscious mind and how it works.

Imagine your subconscious as a behind-the-scenes assistant in your brain, quietly running the show using everything you've experienced before. It doesn't stop to question whether a belief is helpful; it simply records whatever you repeat the most and makes it your default setting. Think of it like a playlist on shuffle—if you keep playing the same depressingly negative songs, they become your soundtrack, shaping how you feel and act without you even noticing.

Then there's your Reticular Activating System, or RAS, a little cluster of neurons that acts like a search filter for your brain. Whatever you focus on, the RAS tends to find more of. If you're always thinking "I never have enough," your brain will show you proof: unpaid bills, scary bank balances, missed opportunities. But if you start focusing on growth, your RAS will scan for that, too. This means if you focus on certain thoughts, positive or negative, your RAS tunes in and helps you notice related things more often, shaping your experience without you even realizing it. This isn't woo-woo or magic—it's biology, the very real and measurable workings of your brain and nervous system.

Finally, your brain is wired to reward repetition. Every time you lock into a thought emotionally, whether it's empowering or self-defeating, you're reinforcing a mental habit. It's like saving a shortcut on your phone. The more often you use it, the faster your brain pulls it up by default. So, if you keep thinking, "I'm not good with money," your brain is fast to serve up more of the same. On the flip side, when you celebrate progress, even small wins, your brain releases dopamine, your feel-good chemical, which helps you build momentum and strengthen a more confident, productive mindset.

You'll see these brain principles referenced throughout the book. They're here to support your Bullshift Process because rewiring your mindset means learning how to use your brain instead of being used by it.

REWIRE ON PURPOSE: HOW YOUR BRAIN LEARNS TO THINK DIFFERENTLY

Your brain isn't fixed, it's flexible. That's thanks to something called neuroplasticity, the brain's ability to rewire itself based on what you think, feel, and do repeatedly. In other words, it can form new connections and pathways as you learn new skills, practice new habits, and adapt to new experiences throughout your life.

Every time you think a thought or practice a behavior, your brain strengthens the neural connections behind it. Over time, those connections become the default, your go-to beliefs, reactions, and habits.

This is good news because it means you're never really stuck. Even beliefs you've carried for decades can be replaced or reshaped with intention. The key is consistency and emotional reinforcement. Your brain isn't just listening—it's tracking what matters based on a few key signals:

- Repetition (how often you think it)
- Emotion (how strongly you feel it)
- Reward (what you associate with it)

That's how mindset habits are formed, not by willpower, but by wiring. And the more you celebrate small wins and interrupt old thought loops, the faster your brain updates the "code."

This may be the shortest neuroscience lesson you'll ever read, but it has the power to change everything.

Now that you understand the basics of how your brain filters information, reinforces beliefs, and rewires itself through repetition and emotion, you hold the keys to lasting change. You are not bad with money, and you are not stuck. Your brain has simply been running an outdated program. The Bullshift Process will equip and guide you to interrupt those old patterns, install new ones, and cultivate a mindset that supports the life and business you truly desire. The Bullshift exercises in this book will help you in the rewiring process, enabling you to achieve the vision that means so much to you.

Let's keep going, one powerful thought at a time.

CHAPTER 4
The Mystery Behind Living a Happy Life, Demystified

After my husband passed away, I continued to work at the beautiful NBC Tower in Chicago, a daily commute of about 90 minutes each way. After five years of being in a constant frenzy, I decided I needed to be closer to home for my now-adolescent girls, so I made the heartbreaking decision to leave my 22-year career in television broadcasting. Since I'd been in the industry all my adult life, I had no clue what would come next for me.

Giving myself a pep talk and a reminder that I had single-handedly coded and managed the first television media website to launch in Chicago, it made sense to build websites for small businesses for a while. It was successful enough, but soon, the workload demand required that I hire additional coders. Let me say that managing them wasn't exactly the highlight of my life. After about a year, I decided this direction wasn't right for me; it was time for yet another career change.

I slowed down on the website work and took the first job I could find. It was a lucrative opportunity, and I could continue to work from home, which was great. Unfortunately, I was also miserable in this new line of work. After a year in my position, I determined it was time for yet another change, and once again, I left a job with no plan. My positive money mindset gave me the confidence to walk away from a six-figure position and all its perks, allowing me to prioritize my well-being and seek happiness elsewhere.

A month or two later, while driving through the neighborhoods near my home, I stumbled upon the most charming coffeehouse. It was love at first sight! Not just for what it was but for what I imagined it could become—a vibrant, buzzing community hub where everyone would feel welcome. It had the potential to be a place where people could gather, enjoy incredible coffee and sandwiches, and soak in the local arts scene.

Several visits later, a ridiculous impulse overcame me, and I approached the owner to tell her I wanted to purchase her coffeehouse. A little negotiating was all it took, and about two months later, on September 1, 2001, I was the proud owner and operator of The Fat Bean Coffeehouse. It was a dream come true . . . until 10 days later, on the morning of 9/11, when terrorist attacks took down the Twin Towers, killing 2,977 people and changing the world as we knew it.

Like most Americans, I watched my portfolio take a nosedive. Mind you, I'd been well-prepared before purchasing the coffeehouse, and I knew I wouldn't be able to draw a paycheck from the business for at least two years. I had set aside enough money for bills, spending, and cash infusions for the company, should they be necessary. My short and long-term investments were my financial lifeline.

But business came to a grinding halt in the wake of 9/11 as people stopped spending money on luxuries, and an expensive latte was a luxury. Soon, my once-satisfying portfolio began to wither away, shrinking with every passing day. What had once been a source of security and pride now felt like quicksand, and no matter how hard I tried to hold on, the financial safety net I had built was slipping through my fingers. I fought tooth and nail to keep my beloved coffeehouse afloat. For a while, things actually started to look up, but by then, I had burned through most of my savings, and my portfolio never had the chance to recover the economy's nosedive. I went from the prospect of an early retirement to barely scraping by.

I had worked hard for that money! My husband and I had painstakingly and lovingly renovated my childhood apartment building, which I ultimately sold. I had taught myself everything I needed to know to succeed in the stock market. I had taught myself coding and basic graphic design so I could build and sell websites. I had stood the test of a demanding career, lived frugally, and invested wisely, all to end up broke because of one wrong decision compounded by one world disaster.

The adverse effects of my naïve choices as an entrepreneur dragged on for about eight years. Every aspect of my life challenged me. At the root of my struggle was an unhealthy relationship, not with another person but with money. My bright and positive mindset, along with my bountiful money tree, seemed like a thing of the distant past. I felt the tug of old fears resurfacing; joy felt inaccessible.

Compounded by the money-related beliefs demonstrated to me throughout my childhood, this traumatic experience left me with images of poverty and ruin. I came to believe that retirement was out of the question, ever. I feared losing my home. My focus turned to making just enough money to get by (as my parents had) rather than rebuilding my wealth. My monkey mind was jumping up and down, grabbing every irrational thought possible, my thoughts shouting at me from the tops of the mountains: *All that money was in your life by dumb luck! You're nothing but a failure!*

"As you think, so shall you become."

– BRUCE LEE

WHEN THE MONEY TREE WITHERS

Engrained thought patterns, whether negative or positive, dictate our day-to-day actions and decisions that impact our future. We limit our potential when we draw inaccurate conclusions about who we are and what we can do.

My once confident and optimistic view of money collapsed when my wealth vanished. My money tree withered and died. The Fat Bean was bleeding me dry, and soon I would become a failed entrepreneur. What would I do then? The skills from my broadcasting career were not transferable to another industry. I was financially doomed.

I blamed myself plenty, but I also blamed my accountant, the economy, and pretty much everything and everyone in the world around me. I bought into every BS story I could tell myself about what a loser I was and how unfair the world was. I had a relationship with myself that was tenuous at best, and my relationship with money had shifted drastically—it was now built upon a series of lies I told myself about my inability and a doomed future.

Have you ever had a failed business? It can feel as though the end of the earth is coming. Embarrassment, fear of what's next, the gut-wrenching guilt of letting so many people down. I wasn't ready to call it quits, so I did what not many people did in those years: I hired a business coach.

Steve was a remarkable coach, and I admired his process and the promise of change that working with him brought into my life. Yet, it didn't do enough to turn things around for me financially.

After about eight months into my coaching relationship with Steve, I had a cathartic realization: It was time to walk away from The Fat Bean. What once felt like my dream now revealed itself as a stepping stone, a vehicle that carried me to my true purpose. I realized I was put on this earth to help others achieve their dreams, to be the guide and champion I had once needed myself. With that clarity, I made a bold decision to become a coach. Before long, I was enrolled in a professional coaching program, and Steve transitioned from being my coach to becoming my mentor as I embarked on a new path that felt deeply aligned with who I was and still am.

Then, as if the Universe recognized my readiness and heard my prayers, two women strolled into the coffeehouse and asked if I'd be interested in selling The Fat Bean. Just like that, it felt like the lifeline I desperately needed. This was precisely how I'd approached the previous owner when *I* had bought the coffeehouse. *Yes!* A way out of the financial mess I found myself in!

What I didn't realize was that these women were about to pull off a scam so blatant it would rob me and deceive my employees, my vendors, and even the government.

A CRASH COURSE IN LETTING GO

As things progressed with the buyers, they were impressed with the coffee house's steadily increasing financials, and I had been open and honest about the numbers. They felt that with a small marketing investment (money I no longer had), they could quickly multiply the revenues. I agreed. The deal was made. With Steve's help, I transitioned into my coaching career and began an entirely new chapter in my life. Letting go of *The Bean* was a very emotional experience, but I was doing a good job of moving on, until the actions of the new owners caught up with me and shocked me back into my old reality.

It was one year after selling The Bean that I received a legal document on behalf of the property management company saying that I owed them nearly $100,000 in back rent and late fees. *What??* How could that be?

I had naïvely sublet the store to the new owners because two years remained on the lease, but now I was being told they had not paid a dime of rent. A whole *year* of nonpayment? Why was I just *now* hearing about this?

As if things couldn't get worse, I was hit with another court summons. The new owners were suing me, claiming I'd misrepresented The Fat Bean's financials! They even accused me of stealing property and breaking my promise to train them on the equipment. Those were all absolute lies. After the sale, I had left every piece of equipment behind and had spent *weeks* showing them the ropes. I'd even covered a few shifts to help them save on payroll.

Still, I found myself in court participating in an emotional and frightening lawsuit, draining what was left of my already-depleted finances. Although I won the lawsuit and was awarded reimbursement of the back rent and legal fees I'd been forced to pay, it was a pointless victory: the two filed for bankruptcy, and I never saw a penny. Later, I found out they'd "vendor-hopped," leaving unpaid bills in their wake, dodged state taxes, and shamelessly exploited young employees by underpaying them or not paying them at all.

That was the final blow—the crème on the espresso, if you will. The last of my money was gone, and so many people had gotten hurt along the way. The depth of misery I felt, second only to the death of my husband, left me shouting with my whole being, how much more could life throw at me?

My mindset was entirely deflated. I spent about three years fiercely struggling with finances. The childhood beliefs I'd worked so hard to change came flooding back:

- I'm not smart enough, good enough, or important enough to make a lot of money.
- Well, we won't starve, I'll have just enough money to get by.
- I'll never stop making stupid mistakes.
- The world isn't fair, so I have to know my place in it.

- People are born into money; it just isn't meant for me.
- We all must work hard, suffer, and make sacrifices just to get by.
- I'm just not unique, so why would I deserve such happiness?
- I should settle and be grateful for what I have.

I spent my days trying desperately to escape this berating voice in my head:

- You should have listened to your accountant and never opened a stupid coffeehouse!
- It was dumb luck that you made so much money earlier in life because you're just a fraud!
- What were you thinking? It was selfish to take such a risk!
- Why didn't you trust your gut? Didn't you know those buyers were scammers? Stupid, stupid, *stupid*!
- You had your one shot at being wealthy, and you blew it!
- You're screwed now, girl! You have *zero* options.

I didn't know that I had the power to shift my BS thinking. The destructive narration was taking me even further down the path to a deep depression and crippling inability to move on.

Then something very powerful happened. I guess the Universe decided it had had enough of my money fears and anxiety, so it forced me to get out of my head and take action.

On a gloomy October afternoon, I received a letter from the bank stating that the line of equity on my home, which I had taken out to finance the coffeehouse (under poor advice, as I could have paid cash), was due. I had to come up with six figures to pay it off, and I had 30 days to do it. By then, my credit was trashed, so they would not renew the line of credit. And even though I'd always been on time with the interest payments, the bank didn't care. I was on the verge of losing my home.

I was utterly traumatized. I became convinced that the girls and I were destined for homelessness; I was absolutely certain we'd be left with nothing. The fear was suffocating. My heart raced constantly, I felt like I could barely catch my breath, and I couldn't sleep. The panic and anxiety were relentless, day in and day out.

But amid that terror, something in me shifted. It wasn't sudden or magical, it was my survival instinct kicking in. At first, it was just a flicker, a tiny thought that maybe, just maybe, I had more control than my fear allowed me to believe. Desperation forced me to seek answers. I needed to find something, anything that might quiet the panic. I devoured books and experimented with mindset techniques I had never considered because they seemed too simple to make a difference. Slowly, I started challenging my thoughts, questioning the absolute certainty of my worst fears. What if, instead of assuming disaster, I could make a different assumption? What if I could rewrite the story before it was written?

Little by little, I leaned into that shift. And in doing so, I found the strength I didn't think I had, and with it, the courage to face one of the most pivotal moments of my life.

THE WORST-CASE SCENARIO

Days after receiving the notice from the bank, I sat down in my sunny office (thank goodness for the sunshine!), took a deep, shaky breath, and asked myself, "What is the worst-case scenario here?" Have you ever had to muster the courage to ask yourself such a question? It's not easy! I had to separate the reality of the situation from my exaggerated fears. Could we—would we—actually become homeless, or were there solutions I wasn't seeing through the murky waters of fear? So, I plunged deep into my darkest thoughts with my heart pounding, my palms sweating, and my mouth dry, seeking the worst-case scenario for every dark thought I possessed at the time.

I listed my most terrible thoughts: We would end up in a homeless shelter or living in the car or cramming into a single bedroom that I would rent month by month on that new website, Airbnb.com. Thankfully, my car was paid off; so surely, I could afford at least that much. Or could I?

As my anxiety became nearly crippling, I took another deep breath and asked myself a different question: "Is that just the BS story in my head, or is it really true?" *Would* we be homeless? Penniless? Forced to live in a shelter or a shabby little one-bedroom apartment at best?

As I persistently questioned my terrifying thoughts, I was led to look at reality instead of the anxiety-provoking BS stories made up by my frightened brain. As I explored the truth versus my imagined reality, it all boiled down to this: no, none of those things would happen. The girls and our little menagerie of pets would move to a small town in southern Illinois to join my mother in her lovely, spacious old home. Whew!

But wait . . . although the option of moving to a small town and, in the process, leaving our friends and the only life the girls had ever known offered some relief, it still sounded awful. We loved my mom, but a rural farming town community? Really? I'm a city girl! I panicked just thinking of this option. We would hate it, or at least I would!

So, I asked myself again, "Is that really true? Is that *really* the worst-case scenario?" Every time a negative thought took over, I started asking myself a simple but powerful question: "Is that really the whole truth, or could it be BS?" I repeated that process over and over, challenging every fear until I uncovered the absolute truth of my situation. I countered each fear, one by one, searching for the brighter side of what I had been too confused and afraid to see. I allowed my thoughts to drift to the potential positives of moving from everything we knew to live with my mom.

- I could put most of my income into savings.
- I would get to be with my mother during what would probably be her final decade or so of being fully healthy and active.
- The girls loved the country and were always thrilled to visit my parents down south.
- I could make the back bedroom, which was beautiful, into a gorgeous office space for myself.
- We would be closer to two of my sisters.
- I could release all my stresses and worries, and we would be safe.
- Without constant stress, I could focus on my girls, my business, and my health.
- I had a business I could grow from anywhere, so it didn't matter if we moved.

I went from full-blown anxiety to excitement and joy within 30 minutes of beginning my "worst-case scenario" exercise. I had options, and in many ways, they were good ones!

Then another amazing thing happened. I realized I felt calmer, was breathing more steadily, and was no longer fearful. I didn't care if the bank took my home away. I felt almost invincible!

As I released my attachment to the outcome, the transformation felt almost magical. Even if life took me in this previously unexplored direction, I had uplifting options and opportunities.

Soon after going through this thought-provoking process, things began to go my way. The bank suddenly and mysteriously found a way to extend my loan. My income increased substantially as my client list continued to grow. Within months, I felt healthy and happy again. I took more classes to better my career knowledge and paid off the bank loan in less time than the financial institution had allowed.

Seeing the profound impact that an intentional shift in my perspective had on my life and business, I dove deeper into gratitude journaling, meditation, mindfulness, the study of neuroscience, and other growth-oriented mindset practices. I stopped saying things like "Yeah, but . . . " to negate any evidence that I could improve my financial situation. I stopped citing statistics to support my negative beliefs, like "Only 10% of coaches make a livable wage, so my odds of success are low." I chose my words carefully until I was fully convinced that I could regain financial independence again. I had done it once already, so why not this time? I wasn't a failure; I'd had a setback. I recognized my negative relationship with money and worked diligently to flip it to a positive money mindset.

Finally, I was ready to be my best self. That was when my coaching practice took off. My faith that the Universe had my back and that my intuition would keep me safe became a guiding force in my life, and it still is today.

During those difficult years, life seemed like such a mystery. How could things turn from good to bad so quickly? Why couldn't I get back to who I was? What was the answer? Where was that magic button? I finally got my answers by letting go of my attachment to the outcome and turning my attention to developing my mindset instead.

> And thus, the mystery was finally solved: the secret to creating a happy life, a thriving business, satisfying relationships, and everyday joy lies in what we believe and how we think.
> **But Who Really Pays Attention to the Way They Think?**

CHAPTER 5

Your First Bullshift: Seeing the BS Clearly

"Your income can grow only to the extent that you do."

– T. HARV EKER

Your thoughts are a catalyst for self-perpetuating cycles, and what you think directly influences how you feel and behave. So, if you fall into the trap I did many years ago and believe that you cannot make enough money to live a comfortable lifestyle or even become wealthy, you'll stay poor. You will make daily decisions that reinforce your negative money beliefs, support your thoughts of failure, and bring insurmountable stress into your life.

Here's the thing: When people have a negative belief system, they don't often realize it because it *is* their reality. If you believe success is hard, you'll think it with all your heart and it's unlikely that anyone could ever convince you otherwise. If you think wealth is reserved for a specific set of people and doesn't include people like yourself, that is your reality. If you believe most people suck, you'll find yourself surrounded by sucky people.

Your engrained beliefs significantly influence how well you attract what you desire, including money. They also affect your ability to hold on to cash and grow your money tree. These limiting beliefs show up in your business decisions. For instance, you might think you can't afford to hire an employee, improve your systems, or invest in marketing. A negative relationship with money can damage and limit your potential as an entrepreneur. In short, negativity certainly influences your access to happiness!

Some people have a positive money mindset and manage to get what they want and more. Oftentimes, though, our money mindset fluctuates between negative and positive, depending on the nature of our focus. Whichever mindset you might currently possess, it influences how well you attract and respond to opportunities for receiving, spending, and saving money. Your core beliefs and attitude about money, and not easy access to money, determine your wealth. Much like what happened to me after my husband died, access to money will come if you believe and trust that it will. Maintaining a positive belief system about your cash flow will inspire your actions and bring just the right circumstances for financial growth into your life and business.

If you believe you can't, then you're right—you can't because you won't. Just as your business started with a single idea, real change begins with a single thought: *Yes, I can!*

Few people sit around analyzing how and what they think, so devoting time to this activity may be a foreign concept. However, a regular practice to gain more awareness of your mindset will change your life.

The Bullshift exercises in this book are designed to guide you on this transformative journey to a more positive money mindset. These exercises have been 20 years in the making! I invite you to experience the transformative power of Bullshift for yourself as we walk this journey together.

Let's begin detoxifying the soil where you'll plant your money tree. In this Bullshift exercise, you'll write down the big, ugly, negative belief or fear that holds you back from the happiness and success you deserve, *and* you'll write down the worst-case scenario associated with that belief. Then you'll ask, "Is this story I tell myself really true?"

Keep deconstructing your belief as I did! Ask that magic question repeatedly until you've converted your fear-based belief into a hopeful one. If you don't have a current big fear or limiting story you tell yourself (and be honest here!), use one from your past.

Before you dive into your first Bullshift exercise, take a moment to take a deep, calming breath. This exercise will help you uncover hidden beliefs shaping your money mindset and begin rewriting the story you tell yourself. Let's unearth the absolute truth so you can embark on the journey to a healthy relationship with money!

BULLSHIFT EXERCISE 1

The story, problem, and/or fear that is probably holding me back is:

____

____

____

____

____

Example: My situation was that I could not pay off the loan, and I believed my girls and I would become homeless or close to it.

What is the worst-case scenario? List every negative aspect of your fear. If this [bad thing] happens, then:

____

____

____

____

____

Example: The bank was going to take away my house, and my girls and I might have to live in the car or in a shelter.

For each negative aspect that you list, ask yourself, "Is this BS, or is it really, really true?" Boil it down:

____

____

____

____

____

Example: I fear we will be homeless, but is that really, really true? Well, no—we could live with Mom in southern Illinois.

Now list the more positive aspects of your solution. You may have to dig deep, but they *are* there! See the list I told you about in my example—it included things like *I'll be able to save what money I make* ,and *I'll be with Mom as she ages*:

____

____

____

____

____

Congratulations on completing your first Bullshift exercise! What insights have you gained? Have you distinguished the genuine truth from the half-truths or falsehoods you've been telling yourself? It's fascinating how our brains can subtly distort reality over time to align with the narratives shaped by our experiences and the limiting beliefs we've formed.

Sure, it's uncomfortable to question the beliefs and emotions you've clung to for years. But staying in your so-called comfort zone may actually be the source of your pain.

STRETCHING BEYOND YOUR COMFORT ZONE

The human comfort zone is a psychological and emotional space where familiarity, ease, and security reign. Within this zone, we experience minimal stress because our environment is predictable, our actions are routine, and the outcomes of those actions feel certain. It's a place where risk is minimized and effort can stay comfortably low, resulting in a sense of safety.

However, while the comfort zone offers a sense of stability and safety, it also holds us back from growth. It's like being in a cozy bubble that shields us from the discomfort of taking risks and trying new things, keeping us from discovering new potential. Staying too long in your comfort zone leads to stagnation. You miss out on opportunities outside of your bubble that bring growth, learning, and real success.

But now we're popping that bubble! We're exploring how to shift your mindsets and embrace risk, step into discomfort, and reap the rewards of planting seeds in unfamiliar territory. After all, we don't really thrive in our comfort zone, we grow and thrive when we stretch *beyond* it.

WHAT SHAPES OUR COMFORT ZONE?

The comfort zone bubble constructs itself over a lifetime and keeps us within an anxiety-neutral existence. Basically, if we don't allow ourselves to be tested by new experiences and new ways of doing things, we feel less threatened and more comfortable. Remaining in our comfort zone means only participating in familiar activities that make us feel "in control" of our environment. Being stuck in that zone means we'll never grow.

Engaging in exercises like the one you just completed can significantly reduce your apprehension about stepping beyond the confines of your comfort zone, especially when a valuable goal is at stake. By consciously examining your negative perspective on a difficult situation and actively seeking more optimistic truths, you'll hopefully realize that the other side of your comfort zone may not be as daunting as you've come to believe it is. In fact, it may hold a world of new and exciting opportunities!

So, the next time you think or say something that increases your anxiety, ask yourself, "Is that a BS story, or is it really true?" Practice it again and again! Soon, this exercise will get easier and become an automatic response to managing negativity. Your world will become a larger place with the success you seek finally within your reach.

Think of it this way: imagine being a kid in a candy store with only two choices of candy in front of you. You've been dreaming of a long candy counter filled with sweet and gooey treats all day long. A choice of only two candies feels limiting, right? That's what it's like when you're stuck in a narrow mindset, operating from fear or scarcity. Your choices are very limited and unexciting. But as you challenge your BS stories and move beyond the confines of your comfort zone, your options expand. Suddenly, that same candy store bursts open with rows and rows of candy in every color, shape, and size! Life becomes deliciously satisfying and rich because your mind is open enough to see and receive it.

The moment you step outside your comfort zone is the moment your money tree gets what it needs to grow. New experiences create new neural pathways, helping you rewire limiting beliefs into empowering ones. With that kind of mindset shift, you are not just growing. You are building the foundation for real, lasting wealth. Now let's explore what that growth can actually buy you.

CHAPTER 6

Money Can't Buy Happiness— Or Can It?

People who are stuck in their comfort zone and possess a limiting money mindset do exactly what I did during financially challenging times: cite dire statistics, tragic stories, and anything else that supports their confining beliefs. The connection between money and happiness is complicated and nuanced, a fact reflected in the long-standing belief that money can't make you happy.

And yet, that belief often becomes a convenient excuse to avoid deeper self-reflection. Instead of challenging the thoughts that keep them stuck, many people use it to justify staying exactly where they are, unhappy, unfulfilled, and financially limited. But what if the real issue isn't money at all? What if it's the way you *think* about money that's keeping you stuck?

If you have a limiting mindset, wherever you go, those limitations will go with you. If you hold many negative beliefs, along with self-doubt, fear, and anxiety, all the money in the world won't change your happiness quota.

Of course, mindset is only part of the equation. How we choose to use our money also plays a critical role in our happiness.

HOW WE USE OUR MONEY—AND THE MINDSET BEHIND IT

Our money mindset and the way we choose to use our money play crucial roles in our overall well-being and happiness. When we use money to meet our basic needs, pursue our passions, create meaningful experiences, and contribute to others, it becomes a tool for fulfillment and joy.

But when we place too much emphasis on accumulating wealth without connecting it to a deeper purpose or balancing it with other aspects of life, money can become a source of stress, emptiness, or dissatisfaction.

Here's where the brain science kicks in. Our brains are wired to seek meaning, not just goals and milestones. Dopamine, the neurotransmitter linked to reward and motivation, spikes when we *feel* a sense of purpose, not just when we hit a specific number in our bank account. If money is used to support values like freedom, contribution, and growth, it can fuel lasting motivation. However, if the goal is simply "more," the brain quickly adapts, and the reward loses its impact.

As entrepreneurs, it's easy to get caught in the trap of chasing revenue for revenue's sake. But when you align your financial goals with a bigger mission and use money to enrich your life and others', that's when your business becomes a true vehicle for happiness and success.

So, you see, the saying, *money can't buy happiness,* isn't entirely true. If your spending habits align with a value-based internal reward system, you will experience more passion and joy in your life. For me, that means helping others, and not only through coaching. I felt tremendous joy when I paid a vet bill for a neighbor's dog because they could not afford it. Donating to causes close to my heart helps me live into my purpose. And, buying meaningful gifts for others probably makes me happier than it makes them! I could do none of these things without the financial resources to make them happen.

THERESA'S STORY

I once had a client named Theresa who founded a nonprofit to provide young Latinas with a beautiful and memorable quinceañera experience. When Theresa was a teenager, her family couldn't afford one. While her friends celebrated in gowns and glitter, she sat in the background feeling invisible and out of place. The experience left her with a sense of lack and disappointment, and it quietly shaped her relationship with money for years to come. She carried that negative money mindset into adulthood and had to work hard to change it. Theresa didn't want other girls to feel the same pain, so she created a foundation that made their dreams come true.

During coaching, Theresa realized that, despite her business booming, she still felt unfulfilled. Something was missing, and she didn't know what it was. We explored what might bring her joy and meaning beyond financial success. She discovered that she hadn't yet connected her work to a larger mission. That shifted when she created her nonprofit. With her purpose aligned and her heart fully engaged, Theresa finally found the happiness she had been missing.

From a neuroscience perspective, this shift was powerful. When we pursue goals that are aligned with personal meaning and contribution, our brains respond by releasing dopamine, oxytocin, and serotonin. These neurochemicals not only boost our motivation, they create a sense of connection, satisfaction, and emotional well-being. Theresa began to feel that shift immediately. Her energy returned. Her days felt lighter. Her work felt fulfilling. For the first time in years, she wasn't just chasing success. She was living her purpose.

THE REALISTIC MAGIC WAND

What brings you joy and gives your work deeper meaning? It's time to pull out what I call your **realistic magic wand,** which means that you set aside limitations and allow yourself to think big! If you had the support you need and the time to focus on what matters most, what kind of work, contribution, or even play would bring you a greater sense of emotional well-being, purpose, and fulfillment, just like it did for Theresa?

Of course, purpose and fulfillment feel even better when your financial needs are met. Money may not buy happiness outright, but it can create the freedom and peace of mind that allow happiness to grow.

Studies show that a higher income *does* increase feelings of happiness up to a certain point. If you can easily pay your bills and enjoy a few of the finer things in life, you'll most likely be happier. On the flip side, if you cannot exist comfortably due to your financial situation, you're more likely to live in a state of stress and worry, and it's nearly impossible to be happy while in a life of struggle. When you are financially sound, it reduces or eliminates your money worries. When you can take a couple of vacations each year, you can detox from stress and experience quality time alone or with friends and family. If you can afford to repair your car and home, join a health club, and wear clothes that make you feel good, your stress and despair will be substantially lower. Perhaps money doesn't directly buy happiness, but it certainly makes unhappiness easier to avoid.

On the other hand, if you *do* have money and your money mindset is skewed, money won't buy you any happiness at all. Theresa quickly realized this as our coaching progressed. Let me share yet another example.

GREG'S STORY

My client Greg inherited several million dollars from his parents' estate. Although he had anticipated the day would come, he was surprised by the wave of depression that followed once the money was officially in his name. He developed a misguided belief that material possessions would make him feel better, so he started to fly through the money by purchasing a vacation home, a $300,000 car, a luxury boat, and other extravagant belongings. However, his depression only deepened. That was when he contacted me.

Through coaching, Greg discovered that he had a significant collection of negative money beliefs. With his permission, I'm sharing them:

- "I didn't earn this money, so I don't deserve it."
- "I still feel depressed, and nothing will ever change that, including money."
- "Because of my parents' wealth, I didn't have a happy childhood—I felt abandoned. I can't let that happen to my kids."
- "All these new possessions thrill me, but the feeling is temporary, so I must be flawed."
- "I have no purpose in life, so I don't deserve this money."
- "Wealthy people have the power to change the world, but they don't, so why have money?"
- "I'll lose it all anyway, so I may as well get it over with and spend it all now."

Greg first discovered his limiting mindset and its hold on him during our coaching sessions. He then realized that just because he *believed* these things didn't make them true. This awareness led us to the next step: to Bullshift his negative beliefs and the way he thought about, well, most everything.

This intelligent and caring man grew in confidence, mentally separating his parenting style from those of his mother and father, learned to believe that he was a good and worthy person, and identified his purpose. Greg became aware of how he could use some of his money and influence to contribute to the betterment of a cause close to his heart: improved medical care for people with special needs. Today, he continues to grow his wealth, cherish his life and family, build businesses he enjoys, and make a difference in his community.

So, you see, your money mindset matters whether you have money or not. It is within your ability to change your thinking, as these clients did, to contribute to a greater sense of well-being and happiness. Then you'll have a fine-tuned appreciation for the money you do have, and you'll attract more of it!

Now that you understand the power of mindset, it's time to take a closer look at how your overall outlook, whether optimistic or pessimistic, can influence both your financial results and your emotional well-being.

HOW OPTIMISM AND PESSIMISM AFFECT OUR POTENTIAL FOR WEALTH AND HAPPINESS

Even if you're a generally optimistic person, it doesn't mean your mindset is open in every area. When it comes to things like money, success, or self-worth, you might still be holding on to beliefs that quietly hold you back.

You may sometimes wonder, "Am I a pessimist or an optimist?" People can be optimistic in one area of life, such as expecting their relationship to thrive, but pessimistic in another, like believing financial struggles are inevitable.

People also may shift positions on the optimism-pessimism continuum as their personal timeline unfolds—we all have "sunnier" days during which we feel happy and hopeful and "gloomier" days when we see the world through a lens of negativity or sadness.

Having worked with countless clients over the last 21 years, I have concluded that more money doesn't change someone who has a strongly engrained pessimistic mindset of scarcity, or at least they won't change without a very deep dive into self-discovery and growth. Pessimists are likely to convince themselves and others that new ideas, changes, and pivoting in business are all too risky due to countless pitfalls and potential dangers. They may think that any efforts to achieve success, financial security, happiness, etc., are futile, so why even try? The pessimist tends to remain firmly planted in their not-so-comfortable comfort zone.

On the other hand, successful people can tap into their more skeptical side to realistically evaluate risk and weigh the pros and cons of their strategic moves. If you're characteristically optimistic, even marginally so, working to expand your growth mindset will take you further faster than it will take the pessimist in the room. Your money tree already has healthier, deeper roots if you lean more toward an optimistic viewpoint, especially when it comes to money and wealth.

A healthy balance of the two psychological dispositions helps an entrepreneur make informed choices and remain grounded while being innovative and confident. Frankly, I don't believe that even those with a healthy, balanced mindset and outlook are pure optimists. Our survival and wellness require a balance between optimism and pessimism, depending on what the situation calls for in the moment. To weigh risks in business, investing, and life choices, it's important to apply some pessimistic thinking. Bill Gates refers to this as "optimistic pessimism."

HOW OPTIMISTIC OR PESSIMISTIC ARE YOU ABOUT YOUR ABILITY TO GROW A FLOURISHING MONEY TREE?

Knowing where you fall on this spectrum is essential because your mindset shapes your actions and results. You may not always realize when your outlook is helping you move forward—or quietly holding you back. The next exercise will help you become more aware of your default tendencies, allowing you to use pessimism as a tool for wise decision-making while staying rooted in the belief that a life you love is within reach.

BULLSHIFT EXERCISE 2

Check Yes or No in response to these questions. If you answer Yes, read and heed the tips following the questions.

Optimism

Am I optimistic to the point of being naïve?

☐ Yes ☐ No

Be more diligent about watching for red flags! Listen carefully to those who may seem negative about the situation instead of dismissing them. Weigh the pros and cons carefully.

Do I have such a high degree of optimism that I become complacent because I believe that one way or another, everything will turn out?

☐ Yes ☐ No

Watch your tendency to leave it to the Universe. *Sometimes it's wise to do that, but if you avoid evaluating your decisions or acting on a problem, there may be a denial-based side to your thinking that's worthy of exploring.*

Do I make poor decisions because I fail to properly assess the risks?
☐ Yes ☐ No

Risk assessment and mitigation may seem like a detailed and laborious practice. If this is a process you're unwilling to go through, find an advisor or a professional in your field who will do it for you or with you.

Do my optimistic ways lead to inflating or overestimating the benefits of an opportunity or a choice?
☐ Yes ☐ No

It's easy to get excited about a new idea when you're an optimist! Create a rule for yourself requiring that you wait at least 24 hours before making a big decision. Also, seek the advice of qualified mentors, coaches, or consultants when necessary. Most importantly, listen to your gut! The biggest mistakes I've made were when I ignored my intuitive instincts because I wanted something no matter how much it cost.

Do I underestimate the time, money, and resources I'll need to complete a project?
☐ Yes ☐ No

This is a big one! How often do you agree to something or make a decision that becomes more complicated than you had imagined it would? The real issue here is boundaries, both with others and with yourself. Again, apply your "24-hour waiting time" rule before committing to most everything, including "small" favors for friends and family.

Pessimism

Am I so negative that I could block opportunities to increase my wealth?

☐ Yes ☐ No

When someone comes up with an idea or you're presented with an opportunity, your inclination may be to say no without giving the matter any serious consideration. Sure, there are some silly ideas, but pay attention to your body—it will tell you if you're shutting down unnecessarily. If your body feels rigid or tense, take some time to evaluate the idea and consider it more carefully.

Do I put others off with my negative statements, attitudes, and viewpoints? Do people often show signs of disappointment or irritation when I make an assertion on a topic I feel strongly about?

☐ Yes ☐ No

You may have strong feelings and beliefs about a few topics: risk-taking, politics, religion, race, how others behave. But remember, extreme opinions come from how you interpret past experiences and may exist to keep you "safely" inside your comfort zone. Also remember that it's difficult (if not impossible) to achieve a healthy vision when you're tucked inside this psychological space of predictability and routine.

Do I give up too easily because I know my efforts won't benefit me in the end?

☐ Yes ☐ No

Base the amount of energy you put into something on the project's viability—don't have an attitude of defeat. Practice greater determination to succeed, including reminding yourself of your ability to succeed. Don't focus on the likelihood of failure!

Do I tend to ruminate and worry so much that I become easily depressed and demotivated?
☐ Yes ☐ No

This problem often goes hand in hand with clinical or situational depression. It doesn't feel good to worry, yet your tendency may be to feel anxious and concerned about things that are totally out of your control. This practice doesn't serve you. If your mind becomes busy with obsessive worry, don't simply think, That's just who I am. *Instead, please consider speaking with a mental health professional. Believe it or not, you have an opportunity to claim your happiness!*

Bottom line? Drowning in doubt or floating on false hope will only keep you stuck, far from success, happiness, and that thriving money tree you deserve. Strike a balance. Embrace just enough healthy pessimism to stay sharp and let the Universe do a little heavy lifting on your behalf.

When you combine practical mindset shifts with a touch of faith in something bigger, powerful things start to happen. Now it's time to learn how that actually works, not just in theory, but through the lens of your brain, your energy, and your results.

CHAPTER 7
The New Science Behind the Law of Attraction

For years, the Law of Attraction was dismissed as nothing more than wishful, woo-woo thinking. Dreamers believed in it while realists rolled their eyes. But modern neuroscience is beginning to confirm what ancient teachings have suggested all along. Your brain responds to focus, repetition, and belief. This is not magic. It is biology.

Neuroscience, the scientific study of the nervous system, including the brain, is now confirming that neuroplasticity, the process of focusing on, repeating, and believing something, can literally reshape your brain. Visualization, affirmations, and intentional belief are not magic or woo-woo; they're mindset tools that train your brain to attract better outcomes. The upcoming exercises will help you to discover this for yourself.

Our brains are constantly processing massive amounts of information. While your conscious mind can handle about fifty bits of data per second, your body sends about eleven million bits to your brain at the same time. Most of that information gets sorted and filtered without your awareness. That's because your subconscious mind can handle an astonishing forty million bits per second. Compare that to your smartphone, which only processes sixty-four bits at a time.

So how does your brain make sense of it all?

That's where the Reticular Activating System, or RAS, steps in. The RAS is a bundle of nerves in your brainstem that filters out unnecessary information, so only the important stuff gets through. But how does it know what's important? It listens to your subconscious . . . and your subconscious listens to your emotions.

The stronger the emotional charge, whether positive or negative, the louder the subconscious shouts, "Hey RAS! Sally really cares about this!" And the RAS responds by scanning your environment for anything that supports or confirms that emotional signal.

Here's the kicker: The subconscious doesn't judge or use logic. It doesn't ask if you want more of something, or if it's good or bad. It just notices how strongly you feel about it. So, if you carry a lot of fear, doubt, or scarcity and those emotions are powerful and run deep, your subconscious flags them as important. The RAS then goes to work filtering your world to reflect those fears right back at you. Not because your brain is out to get you, but because it thinks it's helping.

Basically, your RAS takes what you focus on and feel strongly about and creates a filter for it. It then sifts through the data and presents only the essential pieces of information. It determines what's important based on what you've trained it to notice. That training happens through both your long-term beliefs and your moment-to-moment focus. If you've spent years thinking and feeling that you're bad with money, your RAS will keep highlighting situations that support that belief. The cool thing is that your RAS isn't stuck in the past. You can start feeding it new instructions right now.

To illustrate how the filtering process works, let me tell you a story. My friend Mary noticed that her husband was chopping wood for the firepit without using a proper chopping block. Mary, a gifted massage therapist, was concerned about her partner's back, so she set out to find a large tree stump he could use as a chopping block to make the task safer for him. She was determined to find the perfect stump: one that was just the right height and just the right diameter.

Most people would have dismissed the possibility of finding such a treasure, as locating a random tree stump in our suburban location is unlikely, but not Mary. She didn't harbor a single doubt that she would find what she was looking for. Each time she walked her dogs, Mary imagined discovering the ideal chopping block, knowing it would appear on her path someday.

It took only a few days and about six dog walks before my good friend noticed a couple of large tree stumps in someone's front yard. They were perfect for her cause. She learned those stumps had been right on her walking path for many years, but she'd never spotted them. That's because her brain had filtered them out as being irrelevant. It wasn't until her RAS created a different filter to allow her eyes to take them in that her brain realized the existence of these two tree stumps, one of which was ideal for her purposes. With the neighbor's permission, that stump found new life as the perfect chopping block.

Once your reticular activating system (RAS) decides what to focus on, your brain begins reinforcing the pathways related to that focus. These neural pathways act like familiar trails your mind learns to follow. The more you think the same thoughts or hold onto the same beliefs, the more deeply those trails are carved.

Picture walking through a dense forest. At first, there are no clear trails, so you forge your own path. Each time you take the same route, it becomes more defined and easier to follow. Over time, it feels like the natural or only option, simply because it's the most familiar. These mental trails are like the neural pathways in your brain; they shape how you interpret the world, make decisions, and respond to life.

Now imagine someone else entering that same forest. Even if they begin at the same starting point, their footsteps may lead them in an entirely different direction. Take your best friend, for instance. They might have experienced similar life events but interpreted them through a different lens. Their thoughts and emotions took them down another path, forming their own unique network of trails.

This is why two people can experience the exact same situation and walk away with completely different thoughts, feelings, and beliefs. Each brain tends to follow its own well-worn path, unless we intentionally carve a new one.

I was once food shopping with a friend who had worked in grocery stores for years. Her experience in the food retail industry had been overwhelmingly negative, marked by long hours, difficult customers, and physically demanding work. As my friend and I went through the checkout line, with her ahead of me, the cashier scowled and spoke in a tone that bordered on rude. Understandably, this triggered my friend's stored trauma from her years in the grocery business. However, despite the cashier's snippy attitude and lack of common courtesy, my friend chose to remain diplomatically quiet.

When it was my turn to check out, I decided to try a little experiment. I smiled at the cashier and asked, "Has it been a really tough day?" She then told me some of the stressful things that had happened that morning, so I understood the source of her unhappiness. Should she have been more friendly? Absolutely. But as I smiled and wished her a better day ahead, she returned my smile and thanked me. Hopefully, an understanding customer cheered her up a bit.

As my friend and I walked out of the store together, she turned to me and said the woman should get another job if she didn't like the job she had. At the very same time, I said that the woman must have had a terrible day, and I felt sorry for her. These were two distinctly different interpretations of the same event because of two distinctly different life experiences. Neither was right nor wrong, just different.

Given our dissimilar backgrounds and experiences, my friend and I each walked away with our own take on the cashier's attitude. That's because, while our brains are incredibly powerful, they don't always process new experiences logically. More often, they lean on stored memories and past knowledge, the information wired into our neural networks, to instantly interpret what's happening right in front of us.

BULLSHIFT REFLECTION

Take a moment to think about one belief you've held onto for a long time. Maybe it's about money, success, your worth, or what's possible for your future. Where do you think that belief started? Whose footsteps might you have followed at first? Perhaps a parent, a teacher, or your cultural environment? Now ask yourself:

What familiar path has this belief carved in your thinking?

____

____

____

____

____

How has it shaped your decisions, feelings, or behaviors?

____

____

____

____

____

Is it still the path you want to follow?

____

____

____

____

____

You do not need to bulldoze the entire forest. Simply step slightly to the side and begin creating a new trail. That small step can lead you toward the future you truly want.

THE RAS SEEKS INFORMATION THAT VALIDATES YOUR BELIEFS

You've been feeding your RAS critical information since the day you were born, all based on your life experiences and the beliefs that come from each of those experiences. Your RAS filters everything through the parameters you set, and what you believe to be true shapes those parameters. If you think you're bad at remembering names, you probably are. If you feel like you're a productive person, you most likely are. If you believe that, in general, people are rude or dumb, you'll encounter many people who will seem to confirm that, or so you'll think. The RAS helps you see what you want to see, and in doing so, it strengthens your beliefs and greatly influences your actions.

When you understand the function of the RAS, the idea of attracting things into your life is not so mystical. I prefer using the term mindset magnetism instead of the Law of Attraction. Mindset magnetism makes the concept more personal, suggesting that we can harness the natural design of our own brains. Through the power of mindset magnetism, you can actualize your financial goals and aspirations. It's not magic. It's your brain, including the reticular activating system, that influences the world you see around you and how you experience it. When you learn to leverage it, your RAS is like a personal success coach built into your brain.

VISION BOARDS AS A MARKETING TOOL

I began my education in visualization practices with a vision board. I suggest you do the same! Most people don't realize that the images on a vision board are just tools, not the goal. The real power lies in how those images make you feel. When you choose pictures that spark emotions like excitement, joy, gratitude, and empowerment, you activate the emotional charge that fuels mindset magnetism. These elevated feelings train your Reticular Activating System to notice and attract opportunities that align with your desires, increasing the likelihood that you'll experience what you've envisioned.

I've included some vision board tips in this chapter if you've never made one. Once you practice working with your vision board regularly, you may be able to achieve a high-level vibration without needing a board. Frankly, it's more convenient to practice your visualization at any time without lugging a vision board around!

A VISION BOARD STORY

I had been coaching for only about a year when *Inc.* magazine approached me to do a weekly blog for their website. I couldn't believe my good fortune! They wanted *me* to offer helpful content to their readership of millions of entrepreneurs! Without hesitation, I accepted the invitation and became devoted to my responsibility to our readers, diligently writing a blog post every week. I made no money as a blogger, but I didn't care. I knew it was a prestigious and meaningful opportunity to help others and position myself as an expert in my field. I was thrilled!

Two years later, I received a call from an editor at *Inc.* asking me to become a paid contributor for the magazine. Wow! I had no idea that was even an option. I remember cautioning the editor that I primarily wrote about mindset, business strategy, and motivation. (Remember, this was many years ago, when the topics I spoke about were not mainstream.) “That,” he said, “is exactly why we want you on board. Our readers seem to like your insights.”

I only had to continue doing what I had already been doing for two years: writing articles that would help entrepreneurs flourish in business and life, with the right mindset. And I would get paid! I was so excited that I never asked how much they would pay me.

That’s when I created a vision board for my business. Using Photoshop, I designed a check from Mansueto Ventures, Inc.’s parent company, written out to my corporation in the sum of $3,500. That would be enough to pay my basic monthly bills. Honestly, I knew I was dreaming, but I wanted to stretch beyond my comfort zone to predict an income from my writing that would support my family’s basic needs.

I also added images representing financial comfort: my home beautifully remodeled and a sanctuary for a yard, a nice, reliable car, an exotic vacation, and a personal check made out to my favorite charity for more than I thought I could ever donate.

Guess how much my first check from Mansueto Ventures was? You guessed it: just above $3,500! It wasn’t long before I owned the new car, made improvements to my home, and wrote that check to the charity. My coaching income grew dramatically, partly because of *Inc.* And partly based on my newfound confidence that I was a great coach. Everything on my vision board came to fruition in a very short time.

WHY VISION BOARDS WORK

As you’ve learned, your brain is always rewiring itself in response to where you place your focus and intention. That’s the power of neuroplasticity at work. Visualization taps into this process by giving your brain vivid, emotionally charged instructions about what matters most.

By assembling images, words, and symbols that represent your goals and dreams, you can craft a powerful visual representation of your desired future. This process not only makes your goals clearer but also activates the subconscious mind, engaging your RAS to bring relevant information and opportunities to your attention. When you spend time looking at your vision board, it reinforces your desire for these goals, engages your emotions, and boosts the focus and commitment needed to accomplish them. Through this combination of visualization, intention, and subconscious activation, your vision board can become a powerful tool for bringing your dreams to life.

HOW TO CREATE YOUR VISION BOARD FOR SUCCESS

Define what success means to you.

Close your eyes and imagine what success looks like, not someone else's version, but yours. What do *you* see? A passport full of stamps? A business that runs smoothly while you take a real vacation? Enough flexibility in your schedule to be fully present for the people who matter most?

Success isn't just about reaching a number in your bank account. It's about the freedom to live life on your terms, whether that means global adventures, quiet mornings, or the satisfaction of giving generously. Think about the images that bring those dreams to life for you. What will tell your brain, "Yes, I made it"?

When selecting images for your vision board, go beyond material gains. Include the symbols of freedom, purpose, and joy that fuel your journey. You're not just finding pretty pictures; you're building a blueprint for your brain.

You can create a digital vision board to carry with you on your mobile device. If you search for "digital vision board tools," you'll find many online resources. Some people prefer to use Pinterest to make it easy.

Alternatively, you can browse magazines to find your images; the internet is, of course, another valuable resource. Then glue your images to a poster board. (I like to use a foam core board for sturdiness.) Enjoy arranging your images in any fashion that resonates with you.

Spend 2 to 10 minutes a day with your vision board.

Like exercising, if you don't do it, it won't work, so keep your board accessible. The first thing in the morning and the last thing at night are ideal times to work with your vision board. That's because if you look at your images before going to sleep, they'll dominate your dreams and pattern your thoughts by embedding the images into your psyche. This provides your brain with the information it needs to filter out irrelevant details and allow pertinent information to come through.

Feel your vision.

Remember, this is the most crucial aspect of visualization, yet it is rarely discussed. Our feelings send strong signals to our subconscious mind, which in turn informs the brain of what we want. Again, your subconscious cannot distinguish between "bad" and "good" emotions; it only knows intensity. Allow your images to generate intensely wonderful feelings, like joy, excitement, happiness, or whatever you'll feel once you achieve your vision. Hold these feelings for as long as you can, but for at least 20 seconds at a time.

Visualize yourself doing the work.

Not only is it important to visualize your success, but it's also important to *feel* your success as though it already exists. Envision it in small pieces: If your marketing plan includes online ads, imagine them performing exceptionally well. Your ads convert and bring you a steady stream of your ideal customers! If your success plan includes building a team that supports your vision, imagine them working together in an office or remotely, utilizing every skill and asset they possess to collaborate toward the same vision and mission.

We know that the brain doesn't distinguish a big difference between an imagined vision and the actual experience of something happening, which is why athletes can greatly improve their performance as they "see" themselves engaging in intense workouts and their bodies growing stronger and more agile. They see, sense, feel, and smell what it's like to win and even break world records.

"But what if I'm not visual?" you may ask. That's okay! The goal of this exercise is to achieve *your* desired outcome. If you can skip all the visualization work, good for you! Use whatever tools work for you to produce strong emotions in your body that reflect the excitement and joy of achieving your goals and ultimate success.

Many people with a strong visual sense may not need vision boards or daily visualization, as they've mastered the art of feeling what they want in their bodies. I count myself among them. When I want to achieve something, whether it's a small task or a bold dream, I generate the feeling of success in my heart, head, and solar plexus. I smile and close my eyes to let those satisfying emotions sink in. This practice works better for me than using a vision board, mostly because I tend to forget to look at one each day.

Don't worry if visualization is not your top skill; feel what you want in your gut, and you will make it happen!

Support your vision with actionable steps.

I always say that The Law of Attraction is nothing without action. We hear stories about people who claim to create a vision board and never spend time working with it, yet still get magnificent results. I won't say they are lying, but the odds of this happening are slim.

I feel it's important to blend vision with action to avoid falling into the fantasy trap, expecting miracles without investing in your goals by following the proper action steps to achieve them. I always suggest to my clients that they either create a goals list, use a customized CRM (Client/Customer Relationship Management tool), or even sticky notes to connect each vision with actionable steps. This may resemble a comprehensive business plan, a detailed marketing plan, or a straightforward structure to follow. This is also a good time to engage a qualified business coach to guide you.

Expect the magic to happen.

Okay, vision boards are not magic, but they can feel magical as changes unfold in your life and business. Have a little fun creating and using your customized board! Try not to associate stress with the process, relax with it, and enjoy the outcome.

We'll leverage your vision board and neuroscience to help you attract more opportunities to bring money into your life. First, let's work on identifying your money mindset and relationship with money and wealth to recognize what may be holding you back from achieving everything you dream about and deserve.

CHAPTER 8

Your Relationship with Money (a.k.a. the Money Mindset)

By now, I hope you're starting to recognize the significance of paying attention to your thoughts, particularly those regarding money. When you set aside doubt and explore your limiting beliefs about money, you may discover that many of them aren't true at all.

WE ALL HAVE A MONEY MINDSET.

Yours may be fixed and negative, or you may have a positive, growth-minded perspective. Often, a money mindset fluctuates, depending on the circumstances. For instance, you may believe you have plenty of money to donate to your church but never enough to buy those beautiful shoes you've had your eye on. Or you might enjoy one or two vacations every year yet believe that you cannot afford a new roof for your home. We all have different priorities, so there's no right or wrong, but I encourage you to take a closer look at your spending habits and the beliefs behind them.

What if you believed you could afford to donate to your church *and* buy those gorgeous shoes? Can you take vacations *and* save enough money for a new roof? What if you believed you didn't have to make sacrifices to receive what you want and need in life?

If you shift your beliefs and change your language about spending and saving, you'll be surprised at what you can afford. Remember, your beliefs influence your actions, including your spending and saving habits.

We'll look at the two money mindsets: a positive one and a negative one.

A POSITIVE MONEY MINDSET: THE FLEXIBLE MINDSET

A flexible mindset (often called a growth mindset) allows for healthy curiosity and exists without strict limitations on what's possible. If you view yourself as someone who only makes enough money to get by, that's who you are. If you instead see yourself as someone who is innovative and capable of producing more than enough money, the issue of lack does not exist. When you remove the labels and realize that these are only beliefs, you can liberate yourself from damaging restrictions and adopt a more flexible mindset.

People who generally see the positive side of things or lean toward optimism tend to have less stress and get more of what they want. Wouldn't you like that to be *you*?

In this next Bullshift exercise, the goal is to determine if you identify with any of these growth mindset qualities. Place a checkmark in front of the statements that describe you best (if any do). Sometimes our viewpoint is skewed when we try to identify our own thoughts and behavioral patterns, so consider reviewing your answers with someone who knows you well and can help you get more accurate results. Face this process with curiosity and a light-hearted attitude and remember, this isn't a test, it's a starting point. Whether you check one box or many, you're simply gathering insight to help you grow from here.

BULLSHIFT EXERCISE 3

- ☐ You usually see possibilities instead of limitations: like saying, "Maybe we can move some money around or increase our cash flow enough to take that vacation this year." versus saying, "There's just no way we can take a vacation! It's out of the question."
- ☐ You know you *will* get out of debt rather than worrying about *how* you'll do it. Or you aren't in debt at all.
- ☐ You don't have extreme feelings of fear and anxiety when you think about money.
- ☐ When an unexpected expense comes along, you either get a little anxious but overcome it quickly, or you have faith that you'll find a way to cover it and not worry at all.
- ☐ You believe that even small steps make a difference and get you closer to your financial goals.
- ☐ You do not view the wealthy as greedy or entitled.
- ☐ You do not experience negative emotions such as jealousy or resentment when you have the occasion to experience others' wealth.
- ☐ You can imagine yourself living a more comfortable lifestyle without diminishing that image with thoughts and comments like, "Yeah, but . . . " or "That could never be me."
- ☐ You can make a purchase without feeling anxious about spending the money. However, you don't spend money as a quick fix to make yourself feel better.
- ☐ You have no doubts or fears about your capacity to save money rather than recklessly fly through it.
- ☐ You are well on your way to your next financial goal, or perhaps you're in a great financial place and doing a good job of maintaining your wealth and stability.

If the statements describe you to a tee, congratulations! You have a sound money mindset! If you don't identify with most of these statements, you could use some help eliminating your money woes, so keep reading because that's what we're here for!

Let's see how your mindset may be limiting you and preventing you from achieving your success and financial goals. Please know that you will peacefully coexist with money as you develop a growth mindset.

A NEGATIVE MONEY MINDSET: LIMITED OR FIXED

People who have a difficult relationship with money often think and act from a place of lack and scarcity. A negative or fixed mindset tends to focus on limitations rather than possibilities, keeping someone stuck in the belief that things can't change. When it comes to money, this mindset creates a set of beliefs that can block both financial growth and personal fulfillment. In the worst cases, it leads to ongoing financial struggle. For entrepreneurs, a negative money mindset often holds their business back from reaching its full potential, or causes it to fail entirely, impacting every area of their lives.

But here's the good news: These beliefs aren't permanent. You have the power to change them.

Let's explore how you currently think and feel about money, so you can begin shifting toward a healthier, more empowering mindset.

BULLSHIFT EXERCISE 4

Here are some beliefs I often see associated with a negative money mindset. Can you relate? Place a checkmark next to any of these statements that resonate with you.

- ☐ I work so hard, yet I still can't make ends meet.
- ☐ I'll never be able to afford a vacation.

- ☐ I'll take what I can get for this project, even if it's not my full rate.
- ☐ You don't understand what it's like to struggle. It's the story of my life!
- ☐ Rich people aren't happy, either, so what does it matter?
- ☐ There's always just enough. That's it—that's my limit. I will never have more than just enough money to get by.
- ☐ I can't save any money—I don't make enough to save.
- ☐ I need to take on this client/customer even though they don't match my ideal client description.
- ☐ I am the victim of circumstances—nothing ever goes my way [placing blame elsewhere].
- ☐ Entrepreneurs are successful only when they know the right people, and I don't have those kinds of connections.
- ☐ I am not ____________ enough [good enough, smart enough, confident enough, deserving enough, etc.].
- ☐ I've failed before, so I know I'll fail this time.
- ☐ I'm exhausted and don't have time to grow my business, but I can't afford to hire anyone.
- ☐ My ______________ [parent, teacher, or someone of authority] told me I would fail or that I don't have what it takes to succeed, and they're probably right.
- ☐ The only entrepreneurs who make it are those who sacrifice everything, I don't want to do that.
- ☐ If I had a lot of money, it would change who I am, and I don't want to be one of those selfish rich people.

That's the short list. A negative money mindset runs deep, woven of restrictive thoughts planted along your life timeline. It is comprised of a unique set of beliefs and fears that will prevent an individual (possibly you!) from accumulating wealth.

How many of the statements in this exercise align with how you think? Even if only one strongly resonates with you, it's enough to damage your psyche and bank account.

Perhaps you have beliefs that aren't on the list at all. The next discovery process will help you identify them.

CHAPTER 9

The Perceived Benefits of a Negative Mindset

Now that you've explored how optimism and pessimism influence your mindset, how visioning fuels your ability to see beyond limitations, and how to identify growth versus limited-thinking patterns, it's time to go deeper. Beneath all these patterns are the long-standing beliefs that quietly shape your behavior, day in and day out. These beliefs may feel comfortable or even logical, but many of them are built on old stories that no longer serve you. This chapter is your opportunity to call them out, challenge them, and begin rewriting the narrative that defines your financial potential.

It's completely normal to feel some resistance right now, especially in the next Bullshift exercise, but no judgment here! The beliefs you're about to examine didn't appear overnight. They've been shaped over time through repetition, emotion, and experience, which is exactly how your brain learns to protect you. But just because a belief has been with you for years doesn't mean it still belongs. This is your opportunity to step beyond the comfort zone you learned about earlier in the book, challenge outdated stories, and make room for ones that truly support your growth, peace, and the thriving money tree you deserve.

Negative beliefs often work against us by keeping our deepest fears out of reach. These can include the fear of failure, success, or anything in between. (Yes, a fear of success is a real thing!) I've worked with many clients who come to realize they hold a limiting, fear-based belief that's blocking their success. One such belief is: *If I don't take steps to grow my business, I can't fail.* These entrepreneurs tend to be reactive instead of proactive and find it difficult, if not impossible, to achieve growth initiatives.

These attitudes serve a purpose; they act as a protective mechanism, shielding people from the discomfort of potential failure and rejection. By staying small and playing it safe, they avoid the vulnerability of stepping outside their comfort zone. However, while these beliefs may offer short-term protection from pain, they also trap people in mediocrity, holding them back from their true potential and the abundance and success they deeply desire.

I say all this not to shame you or anyone for having such beliefs, but instead to urge people to recognize them, understand their roots, and gently dismantle them to make room for a growth-oriented, empowered mindset. And since you're here, I'm guessing you're ready to do the Bullshift work to strengthen your mindset and stop hiding behind thoughts that hold you back, just like my client Katherine did.

KATHERINE'S STORY

Katherine took over her parents' business when her father retired. Although she had worked for her dad for a few years, she had not fully recognized the challenges of running a five-million-dollar business. When Katherine began working with me, she admitted that, given what she already knew about the family business, she had made "stupid" decisions and far too many mistakes. While she was willing to admit to those mistakes, she was also very defensive about them and tended to blame others or circumstances she couldn't control.

Katherine had her products manufactured in China. During one of our sessions, she told me she had received a notice from the U.S. Customs Office saying that her Security Deposit Ledger (money kept in holding) had to be increased by $40,000 in three months. Katherine was so stressed out about money that she couldn't deal with the notice right away and put it aside to resolve later. Then she forgot it existed. Three months later, Katherine was in a crisis situation because her inventory shipment from China would be held at customs until she added the $40,000 to the holding account. She was furious with customs and blamed them for the horrible situation she was now in. But had she acted on the initial notice immediately, she could have made money-saving decisions and obtained the necessary funds for the holding account. However, that didn't matter. In Katherine's eyes, it was still not her fault.

During the early stages of our coaching, Katherine continued to make mistakes and exercise poor judgment in many cases. She would then blame customs, the economy, her wholesale customers, her employees—just about anyone she could point a finger at. Katherine's mindset, including her money mindset, was entirely negative.

As time passed, we discovered something important about her limiting mindset and why she frequently made such egregious errors in judgment: Katherine had a deep-seated fear of letting her father down, of demonstrating that she was less capable and less of an entrepreneur than he'd hoped she would be.

"Then why the oversights and mistakes?" you might be asking. Here's why.

Katherine's subconscious was acutely aware of her fear of disappointing her father, so it protected her. Believing that failure was inevitable on some level, she engaged in self-sabotaging behaviors. Subconsciously, she reasoned that if she made mistakes that allowed her to blame others or external circumstances, then the failure she predicted wouldn't be her fault. How *could* it be? After all, she couldn't change customs regulations, the economy, or her customers' buying habits.

Katherine's deep-rooted fear was that the business her dad had worked so hard to grow would crash and burn under her management. The fear of letting her father down and the resulting stress were so deeply embedded that Katherine made reckless mistakes and decisions, then pointed the finger elsewhere rather than take responsibility and learn from her missteps.

As we continued working together, my client grew in confidence and overcame her fear of letting her dad down, which reduced her stress and improved her decision-making skills. She learned to have confidence in herself, take responsibility for her choices, and lower her stress levels. Her self-growth efforts rewarded her with a positive money mindset, allowing her to make better choices and gain clarity on the big picture and the path to success.

Now it's your turn to pause and reflect.

What fears, thoughts, or limiting beliefs consistently hold you back in a specific area of your life?

Ask yourself: What internal criticisms or outdated beliefs are standing between you and the income or impact you desire? Maybe you fear disappointing someone important to you, like Katherine feared letting down her father. Or perhaps you've internalized the belief that success is only for others, not for you.

This next Bullshift Exercise invites you to get radically honest, but also curious and compassionate. Don't worry if this feels unfamiliar or even uncomfortable. That just means you're on the edge of growth.

BULLSHIFT EXERCISE 5

List at least three beliefs or old stories that may be keeping you stuck.

1. ______________________________

2. ______________________________

3. ______________________________

PART TRUTH, PART MYTH

Nice work on that exercise. You may have just uncovered the core beliefs that have been quietly limiting your financial growth and personal fulfillment. Later in the book, we'll work on rewriting those old narratives so you can open your mind—and life—to far greater possibilities.

Before we do that, let's take a closer look. You may already be noticing how easily negative thoughts and beliefs can *feel* true, even if they're not entirely accurate. Sometimes, these beliefs are rooted in real experiences or facts. But the conclusions we draw from those facts? That's where the problem lies. We tend to cling to these conclusions, justify them, and even try to convince others that we're right. Once those beliefs take hold, we stop questioning them. They settle in, limit your choices, and cloud your judgment. Like rotten fruit on your money tree, they can block the growth you've worked so hard for.

Let's explore this idea together. I've included a few examples of what I call "partial truths" below. Use them to guide your thinking as you complete the next worksheet. This time, instead of asking yourself, *"Is this true?"* try asking, *"Is this completely true?"* You might be surprised by what you find.

EXAMPLE STATEMENTS:

- I often feel overwhelmed and struggle to stay focused. (Probably true.) I'll never gain clarity or accomplish what I need to for success. (Not true.)
- COVID devastated my business (this may be true), and I may never be able to get back to where I was. (This is not necessarily true.)
- Things haven't gone as smoothly as expected (this may be true), so I know I'll just keep failing. This can never work! (This is not necessarily true.)

- I don't have a formal business education. (Probably true.) Because I don't have a formal business education, I'll never be as successful as others. (Not necessarily true.)
- I'm an introvert and don't enjoy networking. (Probably true.) Since I don't like networking, I'll never make the right connections. (Not necessarily true.)
- No one I've hired does things the way I want them done. (This may be true.) That means I must do everything myself. (A total myth.)
- I'm good at what I do, but I hate sales. (May be true.) Since I'm no good at sales, there's no way to get new customers/clients and grow my business. (Not necessarily true.)
- I know that my clients are difficult (may be true), but I can't just get rid of them, so I'm stuck working for people I don't like. (Not necessarily true.)
- People may think I know what I'm doing (probably true), but I got here out of sheer luck. (Definitely not true.)

If any of the above examples hit home, feel free to add them to your worksheet as you explore your own part-truth/part-lie beliefs. Use them as a springboard. Dig deep to get ready for planting your healthy money tree. The more honest you are, the more power you'll have to shift what's keeping you stuck and grow a more empowered money mindset.

BULLSHIFT EXERCISE 6, PART ONE

What negative thoughts and beliefs are you willing to consider as only partial truths? Can you list three or four of them? Break your statements in half as I did in the above examples. Like this:

Belief Part 1:
I struggle to stay focused. (Probably true.)

Belief Part 2:
If I can't focus, I'll never be productive or successful. (Not true.)

Belief #1:
Part 1. Possibly true: ______________________________

____

____

____

____

Part 2. Perhaps not so true: ______________________________

____

____

____

____

Belief #2:
Part 1. Possibly true: ______________________________

____

____

____

____

Part 2. Perhaps not so true: ______________________________

____

____

____

____

Belief #3:

Part 1. Possibly true: ______________________________

____

____

____

____

Part 2. Perhaps not so true: ______________________________

____

____

____

____

Belief #4:

Part 1. Possibly true: ______________________________

____

____

____

____

Part 2. Perhaps not so true: ______________________________

____

____

____

____

Pause and reflect.

Look back at the part-truth statements you just uncovered. That kind of self-honesty takes courage, and it's a big deal, so let's keep going.

What do these beliefs cost you? How have they shaped your decisions, held you back, or kept you from trying something new? Take a few moments to sit with that awareness. These beliefs may have started as a way to protect yourself, but now they're just keeping you stuck.

BULLSHIFT EXERCISE 6, PART TWO

Write a short reflection (3–5 sentences) for one of your limiting beliefs:

How has this belief influenced your choices or behavior?

____

____

____

____

What opportunities might you have missed because of it?

____

____

____

____

What would your life or business look like without this belief?

____

____

____

____

You've just uncovered some beliefs that are part-truth, part-myth. Great work! Now, let's take it further and convert one of those BS stories into something far more helpful and grounded in truth.

Let's walk through an example first, so you can see what this process looks like in action. This is a BS belief I mentioned earlier that comes up a lot for entrepreneurs:

> *I often feel overwhelmed and struggle to stay focused.* (Probably true.) *I'll never gain clarity or accomplish what I need to for success.* (Probably not true.)

When we rephrase this half-truth with a positive insight, it might look something like this:

> *I often feel overwhelmed and struggle to stay focused.* (Possibly true.) "Yet, I managed to focus on my studies in school and did well."

Other more optimistic replacements for, *I'll never gain clarity or accomplish what I need to for success* could be:

- When I eliminate distractions, I can think more clearly and accomplish tasks more efficiently.
- When I'm with a client, my focus is great.
- When I talk about my goals out loud, it helps me gain clarity.
- I've come this far in my success; nothing can stop me from reaching the next level.
- My clients are consistently pleased with the results they achieve with us.
- I know what to do and how to do it when I set my mind to something.

Now it's your turn: Write down the big, ugly, BS lies you tell yourself, along with as many statements as you can think of that contradict or weaken that negative belief.

My BS Belief	**Evidence that Contradicts or Weakens My Belief**
I'll never gain clarity or accomplish what I need to for success.	*When I eliminate distractions, I can be clear-headed and get things done.*

Sit with what you just uncovered. Breathe in the truth, that you are capable and deserving!

The next step is to look more closely at what's true.

EXPLORE THE EVIDENCE

One of the sneakiest ways limiting beliefs stay alive is by making you forget your wins. You've probably proven those old stories wrong more often than you realize, but your brain didn't record the evidence. That changes now. It's time to start collecting real proof that you are more capable, resilient, and deserving than those outdated beliefs suggest.

When my coaching clients doubt themselves or stubbornly refuse to believe that their unfavorable circumstances can change, I encourage them to distinguish the false stories from the truth in the stories they tell themselves.

To build the confidence we need for greater success, it helps to rewrite the untruths we've stored in our minds. This allows the brain to create a new library of evidence that reinforces a more positive and empowering mindset. This is neuroplasticity at work!

When I started out as a new coach, I frequently questioned my ability to help entrepreneurs find clarity, achieve their goals, reach their dreams, and live a happy life. I found plenty of reasons to believe the recorded loop of negativity that played repeatedly in my monkey mind! I told myself I lacked sufficient experience as a coach; I had a failed business prior to becoming a coach, and I didn't have the necessary tools in my arsenal to help someone become the successful entrepreneur I knew they could be. *There are many more qualified coaches out there,* I told myself. I knew this habit of negative self-talk had to change if I wanted to become a better coach and achieve my goals.

After about a year of this mental struggle, I finally turned to an exercise I often recommend to my clients, and although it took time and patience, it worked for me too. This process helped me rebuild my confidence and rewire the old, demeaning script my brain had been stuck on for far too long. I systematically gathered real-world evidence that supported a healthier, more empowering belief system about myself and my abilities.

Little by little, I built a case for myself by gathering proof that I was capable, accomplished, and deserving of success. For instance:

- Each time a client verbally thanked me for helping them, I wrote down the words of thanks and acknowledgment they'd offered.
- Whenever my editor at Inc.com or a reader praised my work, I put a copy of their praise in a digital file.
- When I received emails from individuals whom I had helped to overcome a challenge, I saved them in a separate email folder.
- I kept a journal of my successes.
- I wrote about my past and current careers, as well as each triumph I could recall. Every "win," no matter how small it seemed, got recorded into my journal of evidence.
- I reminded myself of how much money I'd made in my past endeavors and how well I had invested it.
- I tracked my clients' success stories and noted how coaching with me had supported each of them in their happiness and success.
- Then I took a big, bold step: I asked my clients for testimonials. Yikes! That was scary, but the genuine praise and heartfelt words they shared became some of the most potent evidence in helping me rewrite my story.
- At every opportunity, I added an uplifting experience as evidence to include in my new catalog.

I used to read these entries out loud and refused to let BS beliefs contradict or diminish my wins. Sometimes, I even looked in the mirror, smiling, as I reminded myself out loud that there were people out there waiting for me, people who needed my help to achieve something meaningful.

GIVE YOUR BRAIN SOMETHING POSITIVE TO PROCESS WITH REFRAMING

Remember, when we tell ourselves positive stories instead of negative ones, our brain responds by strengthening neural pathways that support confidence, motivation, and resilience. It's like giving your brain a pep talk that it listens to attentively. Positive self-talk activates the parts of your brain that help you think clearly and solve problems, while calming down the fear center that usually pumps the brakes on progress. A little kindness toward yourself really does go a long way.

This inner dialogue doesn't just change your outlook; it also changes your chemistry.

You've probably heard of the "feel-good" neurotransmitters, dopamine and serotonin. Neurotransmitters are chemical messengers that transmit signals in the brain and nervous system. When you use positive reinforcement, like affirmations or self-encouragement, you can trigger the release of these neurotransmitters. This not only lifts your mood and motivation but also helps strengthen the brain's reward pathways, making it easier to build lasting, positive mindset habits over time. This shift eventually rewires our thought patterns, making optimism and self-belief more automatic while weakening the pathways that fuel doubt and fear. It's a powerful result of a simple, but not always easy, exercise!

Be sure to build your own library of evidence that supports a positive, supportive, and exciting mindset, which allows you to build your business and wealth. Collect affirmative statements, journal about your achievements and client success stories.

CHANGE YOUR MIND, CHANGE YOUR LIFE

How do you feel after debunking your mindset myths? Even the slightest shift in perspective can create momentum. That spark you feel is the beginning of something powerful! Let's make these feelings into a clear and compelling visualization, shall we? Why? Because, as we discovered in previous chapters, visualization is not just a feel-good exercise; it's a powerful, neuroscience-backed tool that can rewire your brain for success.

When you vividly imagine yourself achieving something meaningful, such as landing a high-value client, doubling your revenue, or feeling truly at peace with your relationship with money, your brain responds as if it is happening in real life. This imagined success strengthens the neural pathways linked to confidence and capability, making those outcomes feel more familiar and attainable. Visualization helps shift your mindset away from doubt and scarcity toward possibility and self-trust. As you continue to see yourself succeeding, you naturally begin to take actions that align with that vision. Your reticular activating system will also start surfacing opportunities and ideas that match what you now believe is possible. That's why visualization is more than wishful thinking. It's a way to train your brain for success. And the timing of when you visualize can make a real difference.

For entrepreneurs with a limited money mindset, visualization can bridge where you are and where you want to be financially. It conditions your subconscious to seek opportunities, embrace calculated risks, and move beyond self-imposed limitations. Instead of focusing on lack and limiting thoughts like the ones you listed in the previous Bullshift exercise, visualization directs your thoughts toward growth: "I am creating wealth," "I am attracting opportunities," and "I am financially free." This shift doesn't just feel good; it changes the way you show up in your business. Your confidence rises, your creativity expands, and suddenly, money-making ideas and opportunities seem to appear out of nowhere. But they were always there. The difference is now you're seeing them since you are instructing the RAS to allow those ideas past its filters.

LET SLEEP DO SOME OF THE WORK

Visualization at bedtime is especially powerful because your brain is highly receptive as you drift off to sleep. Your mind transitions from beta waves (active thinking) to alpha and theta waves—states linked to deep relaxation, creativity, and heightened suggestibility. This is when your subconscious is most open to new ideas and beliefs, making it the perfect time to reinforce positive money thoughts and reprogram limiting beliefs. Over time, these nightly visualizations can reshape your thought patterns, making financial growth and opportunity feel natural because, to your brain, it's already happening.

Understanding the power of bedtime visualization is one thing. Experiencing it in the trenches of real life is another.

BEFORE I COULD TEACH IT, I HAD TO LIVE IT. AND TRUST ME, I DIDN'T MAKE IT EASY ON MYSELF.

Like most new coaches, I struggled as I attempted to grow my coaching practice many years ago. How could I make enough money without exhausting myself by seeing 20 to 30 clients in one-to-one sessions? How could I even *get* 20 to 30 clients? And, certainly, I couldn't raise my fees because the entrepreneurs I loved to coach couldn't afford more! (That's what I told myself anyway.) As I fought my way through this struggle, I cried, begging the Universe to help me find the answers! The stress and worry were killing me! I even took a part-time job, which I hated, but saw no other way.

Finally, an idea occurred to me while reading a blog about visualization. I decided to write a request to the Universe (call it a prayer if you prefer), asking for clarity on how I could continue to pursue the coaching career I loved and earn more than enough to support my family. Before resting my head on the pillow and closing my eyes each night, I read my note to the Universe. I meditated while visualizing my life as a financially successful coach. I applied an essential oil, aptly named Clarity, to my forehead and at the base of my skull. "Why not?" I thought. The scent reminded me of my goal to achieve financial security.

It took me precisely three nights to receive my answer. One morning, I sprang up from my pillow, probably with a shocked look on my face, and said, "I have the answer, yes, yes, yes!" I knew exactly what to do and would do it that day!

Somewhere in my sleep, the truth surfaced. Everything could shift with one decision: to think differently. If my clients valued and benefited from coaching as much as they claimed, they could afford to pay more! I was suffering while my clients were thriving! That didn't make sense.

MY SOLUTION REQUIRED THREE STEPS:

1. Change my limited mindset to a growth mindset and believe in my value.
2. Increase my fees by 125%. (Yes, you read that right.)
3. Charge new clients for a full year of coaching upfront. (I was tired of working with people who weren't committed to the process.)

If this whole idea doesn't sound crazy enough, I landed my first full-paying, committed client the very next day. And another the following week! I made more money in two weeks than I had in the previous nine months!

This life-changing event occurred many years ago, but I still marvel at the sudden shift in my confidence. From the moment I woke up to my new revelation, I had zero doubt this strategy would work and no fear about presenting my new business model to prospects. I possessed not an iota of self-doubt. It's as though a *seed of knowing* was planted in my heart and brain.

More clients followed, and more after that. With my new business model in place, I could coach just a handful of clients and match the six figures I'd earned in my previous career. And it allowed me the time to work on my other endeavors, so my life became filled with purpose and prosperity!

WHAT BELIEF STANDS IN THE WAY OF EARNING MORE MONEY IN YOUR BUSINESS?

What are the thoughts that limit you from achieving your financial goals? Hopefully, you've identified some of them by doing the Bullshift exercises.

My biggest block was the belief that my ideal client could not afford to pay significantly more for coaching. These people were struggling; how could I ask them to pay thousands of dollars to work with me? Until I had my epiphany, the real question buried in my subconscious was, *was I worth thousands of dollars more?*

Unearthing the mental block that's keeping you stuck is life-changing. Now that you've named your problem or mental blocks, write your own note to the Universe requesting clarity and confidence. It could look something like this:

Dear Universe/or God, Higher Self, Angels, Guides, and Loved Ones (Choose what best suits your beliefs.)

Help me remove all that blocks me from achieving success, wealth, and happiness. Bring me clarity and let me see my truth. Give me the answers that will allow me to grow my business with confidence, ease, and grace, and to find the joy, success, and happiness I deserve.

Thank you, Universe!

WRITE YOUR OWN NOTE TO THE UNIVERSE.

Mini Bullshift Journaling Prompt:

Dear Universe,

____

____

____

____

____

____

____

____

____

____

____

____

____

____

____

____

Read your clarity prayer every morning and at bedtime. Sit or lie in a relaxed position. Close your eyes and visualize yourself having received the answers outlined in the request to the Universe that you've created. Imagine that you now have confidence and clarity, and your business is growing. Your mindset has shifted in a positive direction, supporting your goals, and your life is moving in a beautiful new direction.

Remember that your subconscious mind only understands the intensity of your feelings, nothing more. It will send a message to your RAS to reprogram its filters and allow the opportunities you imagine to reveal themselves.

Research on neuroplasticity shows that new thought patterns can begin to take hold in as little as 21 days of consistent repetition. Be patient and persistent. Your brain is listening. Some people notice subtle shifts within a few days, while for others it takes a few weeks of consistent practice. Trust your pace. The results are building, even when you cannot see them yet.

CHAPTER 10
Think You Can't Do It? Change Your Mind!

When you uncover your limiting beliefs, you give yourself the power to change your life from the inside out. That is the heart of the disruption phase in the Bullshift journey. By identifying and questioning the subconscious patterns that have been running the show, you create space for change. As we move into the rewiring phase, you will begin to replace those limiting beliefs with new ones that support your growth, confidence, and financial success. This is the turning point where mindset work becomes life-changing.

RUBY'S STORY

One of my past clients, Ruby, experienced this transformation in a deeply personal and financially significant way. This client was a delightful, intelligent woman. She had owned her business for seven years and earned an average gross income of about $120,000 annually. However, due to overhead, Ruby took home a whopping $28,000 for all her work and dedication. She was miserable and overwhelmed.

It was not lost on me that Ruby had a near perfect business model, which had the potential to grow into the millions, so why didn't she take it there? Within three sessions, I discovered why:

Ruby felt undeserving of wealth and incapable of what she saw as her ultimate success.

Mind you, this client held a Ph.D. and had years of experience in her field. She had a brilliant business model and was dedicated to her employees and clients. The problem was that she promised herself that once her business reached the million-dollar mark, she would become a public speaker, taking to the stage to teach other women of color how to overcome systematic inequality and build a successful business. It was this goal, we discovered, that created self-sabotaging behavior in Ruby, which meant her business grew stagnant. As we dug deeper into her self-sabotaging patterns, we learned that despite her Ph.D. and years of expertise, Ruby felt undeserving and incapable of not only achieving success but also sharing her knowledge to benefit others. There was a deep-rooted sense of inadequacy that overshadowed all her brilliance and hard work.

I'll never forget the day when I challenged Ruby to dig deep to discover her most self-sabotaging belief: I asked her to imagine herself in front of her audience. *What thoughts surfaced*?

There was silence, then tears. "I will be in front of my audience but have nothing of value to say," Ruby said softly. That was her breakthrough: realizing that the barrier to her success wasn't a lack of skills or opportunities but rather a lack of belief in her own worth.

Wow! Ruby's false narrative, combined with the poverty-minded beliefs she learned in childhood, had kept her trapped in misery throughout her adult life. How could someone so intelligent and amazing believe that she had nothing valuable to share?

Once we made this important discovery, we worked on building up her confidence and reprogramming her money mindset. Using many of the concepts in this book, Ruby formed a new opinion of herself and her abilities, and within six months, her business hit the million-dollar mark. Within four years, it hit *$40,000,000!* And

Ruby didn't just speak to audiences from the stage—she went on to appear on *The Today Show* and launched another company, which included a reality TV show. Her new venture was built on the belief that improving individuals' self-worth, work readiness, and employability skills, regardless of their background, would create more job opportunities for them. Now, Ruby is a published author many times over and is living the life she'd imagined! All because she changed her mind. She learned to believe in herself, her worth, and her ability to attract wealth.

THE ROOT OF LIMITING BELIEFS

Now that you've done the work to recognize some of your own limiting money beliefs, let's take a deeper look at where they came from, because you certainly weren't born with them!

Beliefs are inner convictions that we all develop throughout our lives, often without realizing it. They form automatically through our experiences and are shaped by family, friends, teachers, society, social media, and other outside influences. For instance, if you grew up hearing negative messages about money or criticisms of wealthy people, chances are those beliefs followed you into adulthood. The good news? Once you become aware of these inherited stories, you have the power to question them and to change them.

From the day you were born, you began having first-time experiences that taught your brain what to believe, how to feel, and how to respond.

These early experiences created internal patterns that influence your reactions today, often without your awareness. Sometimes your responses won't make sense, not even to you. That's because neural pathways are formed through repetition and emotion, not conscious choice. The environment around you, combined with repeated feelings and events, silently shape your brain's wiring. These pathways lead to automatic responses and beliefs, even when you don't understand why you react a certain way. You may behave in ways that feel out of place or irrational, but they are rooted in your brain's early programming. This programming was set before you were able to understand or question your thoughts. Parents often see this in their children, as my husband and I did.

THE ICE CREAM PHENOMENON

It wasn't until our twin girls were about three years old that they first encountered an ice cream sundae. I was never a big ice cream fan (I know, that's strange), so the idea of feeding my children ice cream or sweets in general had never occurred to me. I remember their first-time experience of sitting in highchairs at the local ice cream parlor, looking as adorable as ever, with no idea of what was about to happen. The server arrived with two scoops of ice cream, each decorated with eyes, a nose, and a big smiling mouth; each was crowned with an upside-down sugar cone. Little clown sundaes!

Kim and Lauren sat, staring at those concoctions, feeling uncertain about what to do with them—but not for long. Wally and I placed spoons in their hands and encouraged them to dig in.

At first, the girls didn't quite know how to respond to the texture and temperature of this silly upside-down clown and his sugar cone hat. Where to begin? I could see their little brains processing all the new information: *Touch it!* It's cold. *Dab it into my mouth!* Oh, it melts. And it's very sweet! But wait—it slides off the spoon if I don't get it into my mouth fast enough! Hurry, eat it before it melts away!

Once Kim and Lauren had processed the taste, touch, and smell of their sundaes, they couldn't eat them quickly enough. But much to our surprise, our little girls did not look happy or pleasantly excited—instead, they were intensely focused on getting this yummy culinary delight into their bellies as quickly as possible. Before we knew it, they were all done . . . and then when we got up to leave the ice cream shop, both girls grabbed onto the table, crying and refusing to leave. They wanted more. Eating ice cream. What most kids would have seen as a routine treat was something entirely new and unfamiliar for my little girls, making it feel like a rare occurrence that might not happen again.

My husband and I were taken aback by their reaction. We didn't want them to carry a negative impression of such a typical childhood joy! This first encounter with ice cream, filled with intense sensory inputs and the immediate emotional response of wanting more, shaped their initial behavior. We didn't want the girls left with that lingering impression, so the next day, we purchased a pint of vanilla ice cream and a box of cones to hopefully normalize this simple pleasure.

Each time we gave the girls their weekly ice cream cone at home, their reaction was the same: tears and tantrums as soon as they finished. This pattern continued for a few weeks, until they'd had enough ice cream cones to ease their fear of returning to a life that wouldn't include such a delicacy. My husband and I were puzzled. What could trigger such a strong, emotional response to something so simple and joyful? It wasn't until years later, when my interest in neuroscience grew, that I finally understood what had been happening.

PROGRAMMING OUR BRAINS

Our brains contain basic building blocks called neurons. There are about one hundred billion of them, and they act as the senders and receivers of information throughout your brain. These neurons are connected by the neural pathways we've been discussing. Think back to the forest path metaphor from Chapter 7. These neuron-packed pathways form those familiar mental trails you've created.

Thanks to neuroplasticity, your brain can create entirely new pathways. Each time you shift your mindset or view a situation from a new perspective, your brain begins to lay down fresh connections.

As you repeatedly see, feel, hear, or experience something differently, that new pathway becomes stronger. Eventually, it can override the old, automatic trail and become the dominant route your brain follows.

Reflecting on the ice cream story, our daughters continued to respond negatively to ice cream since it was a shocking first-time culinary experience. (That didn't speak well for my cooking!) For some reason, they feared they would never have the chance to eat this foreign food again. Fortunately, by offering them a repeat experience, we reprogrammed the neural pathway that had shaped the belief that ice cream would be a one-time experience. Over time, their neural pathways adapted, making ice cream a normal part of their experience rather than something extraordinary or scarce. Their repeated exposures helped create new, more positive neural connections, successfully shifting their emotional responses through repeated positive exposures to ice cream.

And that's just a very basic example of how neural pathways that don't serve us well are formed! Can you imagine how a serious trauma must affect us in the long term?

I've worked with many individuals over the span of my career who have experienced heart-wrenching tragedy. Whether in childhood or adulthood, these stories often come with deep emotional wounds, limiting beliefs, and lingering guilt that shape how they see themselves and what they believe they deserve. While we can't rewrite the past, we can absolutely rewire how the brain interprets it. With care, intention, and the right tools, it's possible to release the weight of these painful narratives and rebuild a more empowered, truthful version of your identity. A version rooted in resilience, worthiness, and growth.

Even in the wake of pain, loss, or trauma, the brain remains adaptable. That is one of the gifts of being human. Your mind can change, and so can your life.

Now that we've acknowledged how deeply engrained beliefs form through difficult experiences, we can take a closer look at how your brain holds onto those beliefs and how you can begin to shift them.

Again, our brains develop these pathways based on our experiences, emotional responses, behaviors, and the beliefs that result from them. The more we use these pathways, believing in and acting upon their messages repeatedly, the more engrained and automatic they become as they settle into deeper areas of the brain. The downside is that by the age of 25, many of these pathways are well established. It can be challenging to break free from them! These learned responses, deeply embedded in our brains, can play on repeat like a broken record, reinforcing limiting beliefs and holding us back.

Have you ever had an experience where you suddenly feel down, anxious, or uncomfortable, but you can't figure out why? Or maybe you carry a fear or phobia that you can't understand or explain? These are examples of your pre-formed neural pathways firing automatically, triggering emotional or physical responses that don't always align with your current reality. Even when those pathways no longer serve you, your brain relies on them because they are familiar and efficient. But just because a response is familiar does not mean it is accurate or helpful. This is where awareness becomes powerful. Once you recognize that these patterns are old programming, you can begin the work of choosing new thoughts, building new connections, and reshaping the way you respond to life.

Once you recognize these patterns as being false or unhelpful, you can begin to shift your perspective toward more empowering and supportive thoughts—about money or any other area of your life. You can raise your awareness and rewire your brain for success, thanks to neuroplasticity. We aren't fully aware of our beliefs until we consciously decide to examine and question our ways of thinking. What we assume to be true might not be true at all. You've already taken an important step by doing the earlier BS exercise, where you separated your false narratives from the actual truth. That practice is your brain's cue to start forming new, healthier connections. Keep going. You're creating real change!

We all carry a mix of beliefs that shape how we experience life. Some of these beliefs help us grow and thrive, while others quietly hold us back or make us miserable. If you're naturally optimistic or have done consistent mindset work, you may lean more toward empowering perspectives. On the other hand, limiting beliefs can easily dominate when we're unaware of the stories we tell ourselves. You explored this in the BS exercise, where you looked at whether your internal dialogue tends to skew more positive or negative. That awareness is key. The more you focus on possibility, the more satisfaction and progress you'll feel with money, and in every area of your life.

It's valuable to know how you developed your limiting beliefs so that you can start unraveling and challenging them, paving the way for new, empowering beliefs that will support your growth and success. Understanding their origins allows you to reframe your mindset, break free from self-imposed barriers, and take intentional steps toward the life and business you truly desire.

Luckily, there are many ways to reprogram your thought process and rebuild your beliefs so that they better support your goals and vision. You've already begun doing this important work through the exercises and insights earlier in the book, and there's even more to learn and apply as you continue on your Bullshift journey.

WHO TAUGHT YOU ABOUT LIMITATIONS?

Do you know who taught you the beliefs you listed in some of the BS exercises you've done thus far? Usually, it's someone we consider to be an authority: parents, teachers, adult relatives, peers, bosses, and the "experts" we see on social media and read about in books.

When I started out as a new coach, I followed every successful coach I could find on Facebook. I thought I'd gain important insights and learn new business strategies that way. However, I carried many beliefs that limited my confidence and created doubt about my ability to succeed as a coach. My brain's programming was hard at work!

I admired the coaches I followed, but instead of feeling inspired, I felt like I didn't belong among them. Their success stories intimidated me; I couldn't imagine myself being savvy enough to build a thriving practice like theirs. As I navigated my complex web of limiting beliefs, my fear and doubt only grew, pulling me back onto the same familiar trails. These well-worn forest paths had been carved during childhood and were later reinforced by my perceived failure with The Fat Bean Coffeehouse.

It's pretty remarkable how easily we form negative impressions of ourselves and others, often without even realizing it. The upside? With a bit of awareness and determination, we *can* rewire that programming. In my case, it came down to changing my mind about how I viewed those coaches. Instead of letting their posts trigger self-doubt and pull me back into old mistakes, I had to take them with a grain of salt and refocus on creating my own success. Still, my internal programming resisted. I couldn't fully make the shift until I stopped following those coaches altogether until I cleared them, and the BS stories I'd built around them, from my mind.

The fear that I was destined to live in poverty (far from the truth!) made me feel like I was holding my breath underwater with no chance of surfacing for air. My negative money mindset blocked my access to self-confidence and gripped my heart with debilitating tendrils of uncertainty. This was the point in my career when I realized I needed more than my coach training to help myself and to provide my clients with transformational experiences.

The early stages of my coaching career took shape as I added educational experiences and tools to my arsenal of skills and strategies, equipping myself to serve my clients better and build a more impactful coaching practice. Each new piece of knowledge and tool I acquired became a stepping stone, allowing me to gradually build my confidence and expertise as I navigated the early challenges of my journey.

This kind of growth begins with recognizing that we are limiting ourselves and that our brain and mindset are not "fixed" but are instead flexible and capable of change. Embracing the idea that our brains are adaptable allows us to rewire old patterns, adopt new perspectives, and create more empowering beliefs that align with our goals. This mindset shift is the foundation for overcoming our limitations and unlocking our full potential.

Now let's work on recognizing *your* patterns and where they may have come from! I'll ask you to reflect on certain aspects of your life, going as far back as you can remember. Do you recall the people and experiences that left you feeling inadequate or with a limiting perspective on money?

I'll give you one of my childhood experiences as another example. When I was 11 years old, my dad became ill and had to stop working. My older sister is a nurse practitioner who lives in Hawaii, and according to my father, she's the authority on all things health-related. (Frankly, she *is* pretty brilliant.) So, when my sister suggested that Dad would recover better if he moved to Hawaii and spent time with her, he did just that.

As a result, Mom had to leave four kids at home alone while she worked a full-time job. That included my younger sister, who had Down syndrome, my younger brother, me, and an older brother who was rarely home. Our older siblings had already moved out on their own.

I unwittingly sacrificed my youth to care for the household and my younger siblings. There was an unspoken expectation that I would cook, clean, and keep the others safe and entertained. I didn't mind—*It's just what a family does*, I thought.

The subconscious conclusion I drew from all of this is that we must all make major sacrifices (including our happiness) just to get by financially. There was never extra money for clothes, fun experiences, or new things. None of us were happy, but none of us complained. My brain translated that to "You suffer in silence."

This was when my lack mindset began to take shape: my childhood experiences taught me that, while I would never starve and I would always have a roof over my head, that was about the extent of it. *Wealth was not in my future*, became another engrained thought pattern—another neural pathway that would someday need to be reprogrammed.

Your money mindset is much like a computer's operating system: it drives many behaviors and decisions. You developed this mindset (along with many other related habits) during your formative years. Your parents likely passed on their beliefs about money indirectly as you observed, listened, and absorbed both the positive and negative attitudes embedded in their thoughts and actions. You witnessed decisions being made or deferred, and perhaps you overheard whispered discussions or even heated arguments.

Awareness of them is the key, because your money mindset is at work 24/7 in your business and personal life! It provides a pathway to making decisions based on your hardwired belief system and how you interpret the available data.

So, here's the pivotal question:

Do you want your mindset and business to be in a different place in a few months or a year from now, or do you want to be fighting the same battles?

If your goals require you to think and operate differently than you have in the past, it's helpful to identify your thought patterns and the source(s) of your limiting beliefs. These patterns often stem from early life experiences and quietly shape your decisions, even decades later.

BULLSHIFT EXERCISE 7

To further understand your current money mindset, answer these 12 questions the best you can:

1. What was the most impactful money lesson I learned as a child?

____

____

____

____

____

2. What messages about money did I hear repeatedly growing up? How did they make me feel?

____

____

____

____

____

3. What were my mother's spending/saving patterns? What about my father's? How did I feel about each of their patterns?

____

____

____

____

____

4. When I was young, did I consider my family to be rich, poor, or somewhere in the middle?

____

____

____

____

____

5. In my family, was money an "issue" and a source of conflict, or was it a tool for achieving goals and experiencing pleasures in life?

____

____

____

____

____

6. When I think about money today, what emotions come up most often?

____

____

____

____

____

7. What did my family's financial situation teach me about who I am or what I deserve?

8. What has been the most important lesson (positive or negative) I learned about money as an adult?

9. In my current financial life, am I more of a spender or a saver?

10. What money habits, if any, have brought me closer to my values and goals?

11. How do my childhood money beliefs show up in the way I run my business?

____

____

____

____

____

12. What money mindset and/or habits have been obstacles to reaching my life goals?

____

____

____

____

____

Take a close look at your answers to these questions. What insights have you gained about yourself? Can you identify patterns or beliefs that influence your decisions, especially around money? How do these underlying factors impact your business goals? Understanding the "why" behind your decision-making will empower you to break free from automatic habits limiting your success. By recognizing these patterns, you can make more intentional choices that align with your goals and move you closer to the financial and business success you desire.

This kind of self-reflection isn't always easy, so take a moment to acknowledge your courage. You're doing powerful work, let's keep going! **The real shift begins here.**

Congratulations! You've stuck with the process and put a lot of time and energy into getting to know your inner self better. While some of this work may already feel emotional to you, we're about to identify something that may strike an even more profoundly emotional chord. Why? Because we need your complete buy-in for this process to work.

You can leverage the self-awareness you've achieved by exploring and writing about your money mindset and all its complexities to help you attract success and abundance. Unfortunately, human nature dictates that we must have a powerful motivator to set us into action and make a strong commitment to change. That motivation comes from answering one crucial question:

What has your limiting money mindset cost you?

We all need a powerfully convincing reason to change. By recognizing the pain, stress, and suffering that result from living in your world of lack, you may find the determination and the "why" behind your need for change.

I've provided some writing prompts to help you discover more about your limiting mindset, particularly concerning your self-worth and your ability to attract sufficient money to your business and personal life. Go deep on this one! Explore every desire, relationship, and corner of your life. With a powerful commitment to shifting your belief system and changing your life, you will overcome your lack mindset.

BULLSHIFT EXERCISE 8

Use these writing prompts to spark your awareness and find your truth. Go on to write about any other areas of your life affected by your financial struggles and the related emotional burdens you carry.

First, identify your current situation:

Currently, I make $_______________ a month.

To cover my expenses, both business and personal, I need to make $_______________.

I/we have been struggling financially for __________ years.

Now identify the sacrifices and cost to your life and business:

I have anxious thoughts about money _________________ [how much of the time?].

These anxious thoughts and worries keep me from _____________ ____.

I am $_______________ in debt.

Debt makes me feel _____________________________________ ____.

At this rate, I will pay off my debt in __________ years/months. [Or never?]

Healthwise, I am in _______________ shape. Primarily, my health issues are:

____

____

____

____

____

My stress level at work is ______________________________ because ____.

My stress level at home is ______________________________ because ____.

As a result of my stress and worries:

Am I hurting someone I care about because of my stress around money and lack of sufficient resources to live comfortably? Who? ____.

I argue about money with ______________________________.
Those arguments make me feel __________________________.
My guess is that the people I argue with feel ___________________.
Unspoken worries about money are present between me and ____.
Those unspoken concerns make me feel ___________________.
Those unspoken concerns probably make [my partner, spouse, children, etc.] ______________________________________ feel ____.

Because of my limited income, I am unable to ___________________ [list everything here: pay bills, grow my business, take vacations, move into a bigger home, repay debts to family, etc.]

If I don't increase my revenues/income, what will happen to [list everything: my emotions, health, relationships, desires, finances, future, etc.]:

____

____

____

____

____

I want to increase my income to ________ by this date: _________.

When I achieve my goals, then ____________________________

____

[what **negative** things may happen?].

When I achieve my goals, then ____________________________

____

[what **good** things may happen?].

Other things I fear, need, hope for, and believe about my current financial, relationship, physical, and emotional states are:

____

____

____

____

____

Whew! Completing these worksheets took a lot of contemplation and honesty. Great job!

Take a moment to really acknowledge what you've accomplished here. You didn't just answer questions; you confronted long-held fears, explored how your past has shaped your beliefs, and began connecting the dots between your mindset, money, and self-worth. You've unearthed truths that may have been buried for years and brought them into the light where they can finally begin to change.

At this point, you've gained deep insight into the stories that have been running your financial life. You've traced them back to their roots and started to understand how they formed. More importantly, you've seen that they are not permanent. You now hold the awareness, tools, and courage to start reshaping those old neural pathways and creating new beliefs that reflect your true potential.

You've reached a powerful point in your Bullshift journey. By uncovering the limiting beliefs that have shaped your decisions, you've taken back control of your mindset and started to rewire the thoughts that once held you back. But mindset work isn't just about shifting thoughts. It also affects your physical energy and the way you move through your day. In the next chapter, we'll explore how your beliefs show up in your body and how to recharge your energy so you can stay focused, clear, and resilient as you continue to grow.

CHAPTER 11
Your Energy Shapes Your Success

Now that you've been identifying and shifting your limiting beliefs around money and success, you're already reshaping the way you think and behave. That internal transformation is powerful, but it's only part of the picture. Your mindset influences more than just your thoughts; it also affects your physical energy. If you've been holding on to stress, self-doubt, or old belief patterns, you may be feeling the impact in your body. Maybe you're tired, overwhelmed, or just not doing the things that make you feel your best. Let's take a closer look at how your brain and body work together and how you can start building energy that supports your growth.

Negative beliefs drain our physical and mental energy. To put it bluntly, a brain that's chock-full of BS beliefs cannot operate at full capacity. Instead, it operates from survival mode, which is 100% unproductive, and it's absolutely exhausting. Let's see what we can do to get you out of survival mode and into your thriving energy!

MEREDITH'S STORY

One of my former clients, I'll call her Meredith, believed that her success and worth were directly tied to how hard she worked, how much she regaled others with stories about her struggles, and how difficult her life appeared to be. She happily shared stories of challenges and setbacks with anyone who would listen, as if her battles in life and business earned her merit points. Stress became her badge of honor, and she wore it proudly, but it left her utterly exhausted, day in and day out.

Once again, we see an example of someone blaming everything and everyone but the real source of the stress and setbacks: Meredith herself. As an entrepreneur, she embraced a sense of martyrdom around her challenges, a label she wore comfortably due to her upbringing as the eldest child. From a young age, she took on the responsibility of caring for her younger siblings, essentially stepping into a parental role by the age of 10. In doing so, she sacrificed her own childhood and internalized the belief that life was all about sacrifice and struggle. Over time, she learned to take pride in this struggle because the idea of living without it felt far too unfamiliar and unsettling.

There was a lot to unpack with this client, who was also going through a difficult divorce and child custody battle. However, with her dedication to self-growth and coaching, Meredith's negative mindset slowly evolved into a more flexible mindset.

Meredith is a loving, giving person who deserves more in her life than battles and sacrifice. We focused on building her confidence and redefining her self-worth. Once she realized that her ideas and discussions about struggle only attracted more of it, my client started journaling, practicing gratitude, and leading her business from her expertise instead of feeling like a victim of circumstance.

Now, Meredith recognizes the weakness she showed by wearing her busy schedule like a badge of honor. She was a victim of her mindset and her business, but not anymore! By adopting a flexible mindset, Meredith and other entrepreneurs like her can reclaim their lives and find greater peace of mind instead of constant stress.

Today, Meredith enjoys a peaceful life for the most part. Remember, life balance is *not* about having peace and balance all day long, every day. No, especially not for an entrepreneur! It's about having a broader perspective on your life and the peace and joy you can experience in the big picture. To help clients like Meredith shift into this broader perspective and truly reclaim their sense of peace, I often encourage them to start with something simple and sustainable. That brings me to a suggestion I share with nearly every entrepreneur I coach:

PUT A LITTLE VACATION IN EVERY DAY.

Okay, I hear you. You may be thinking, *Who has time for breaks?* The reality is that you cannot afford not to take them. Stepping away from your work restores clarity, lifts your energy, and actually makes you far more productive. A clear mind makes fewer mistakes and moves through tasks with more ease and efficiency. Forcing yourself to grind for hours without rest drains your focus, slows your progress, and takes a toll on your mood and health.

Research shows that the human brain needs a break at least every two hours. After that point, productivity begins to decline sharply. In other words, working nonstop is not a sign of discipline; it's a recipe for exhaustion and diminished results.

When I worked at NBC, I had a long commute to look forward to daily. From start to finish, it was about 90 minutes each way! But honestly, it was valuable "me time" since I had two young children and a pre-teen stepdaughter at home, not to mention an exasperating mother-in-law. That said, my commute was also an exhausting, time-sucking part of my life. Sometimes, I felt so trapped because I rarely had a moment to relax and have fulfilling experiences outside of work and raising my daughters. I remember thinking to myself that as soon as I stepped out of my house in the morning, I belonged to my job, and as soon as I set foot in my home at night, I belonged to my family. When could I feel like I belonged to *myself*?

One day, I was about 20 minutes early for my train into the city. It felt refreshing not to have to run from the parking lot to hop onto the waiting train. I decided to walk across the street and get a cup of coffee from a charming little coffee shop I had never visited, although it had been there for years. Inside, there was a line of about 10 people, all happily chatting and smiling. The two owners were behind the counter, furiously working to fill the orders, all while making jokes and greeting their customers by name. The moment I stepped through those doors, I felt like I was on vacation in a breathtaking seashore town somewhere out east.

After sharing a few laughs with the other customers, I carried my delicious cup of coffee to the small park in front of the station and sat on a bench facing away from the busy train platform. Then, I intentionally focused on anything but work, the kids, and my stress. I noticed squirrels playing, chasing their tails, and spinning around the tree trunks as if they were doing a maypole dance. I saw tiny violet flowers blooming in the grass and realized how the scent of lilacs filled the air. Such calming, cheerful things—things I had never noticed before. How could that be? These precious moments changed my day because I felt like I was getting meaningful "me time" before immersing myself in my job.

From that day forward, I set the intention that I would put a little vacation into each day. Even on a day with back-to-back clients and only 5 to 10 minutes in between appointments, I still take five minutes to enjoy my backyard koi ponds and the soothing sounds of the waterfall bubbling over the rocks. I see the sun glistening on the pond and the koi frolicking (do fish frolic?) in the cool, crisp water. I see and smell the vibrant blooms that I arrange in large pots in the spring. And I breathe . . . I just breathe.

Other things I might do include taking my lunch to the forest preserve and simply eating in my car while looking over the lake; going to the coffeehouse to read a chapter or two of a juicy novel; or just taking a walk in the woods or at the prairie. When I worked in the city, I would do a quick run to somewhere like the historic and beautiful Marshall Field's, may it rest in peace. Sometimes I would take a nice run by Lake Michigan at lunch.

My little vacations re-energize and refresh me so I can perform at my best for my clients and maintain high energy levels for myself. It improves my receptivity, allowing me to be in a flow state with my clients and in my writing.

Even just a few minutes alone can revive your energy and improve your focus. Your little vacation can help you be more receptive and positive in your viewpoint! On the opposite end of the spectrum, exhaustion and stress will deplete your ability to be optimistic and devote energy to focus on what you *want* rather than on what you lack. So, when you are busy pushing yourself beyond your limits, remember this:

Healthy practices like putting a little vacation into every day will give you a mini taste of the freedom you crave. Your micro-vacations of 10 to 30 minutes will also help you avoid exhaustion, achieve clarity, become more productive, and appreciate life.

Even if you don't have a koi pond or a prairie nearby, there's always an opportunity to steal away for a few minutes, and I don't mean a cigarette break! Do something that feels uplifting and healthy for your mind. This may sound like a small contribution to growing your mindset but remember that the steps toward a growth mindset are simple, but not always easy.

MINI BULLSHIFT JOURNALING PROMPT:

To make your micro-vacations hassle-free, list three or four ideas to refer to when it's time for your escape. What can you do to create refreshing moments in which you can be still and feel gratitude and peace?

Jot down a few ideas here:

____

____

____

____

____

____

____

____

____

____

YOUR BRAIN DOESN'T THRIVE ON COFFEE ALONE

You're already doing the work to rewire your beliefs and shift your mindset. That takes focus, determination, and energy. But if you're still feeling foggy or depleted, it may be a sign that your brain needs more support from the outside in.

So now, let's look at what your body needs to keep up with the work your mind is doing.

Your brain works a lot like your Money Tree. If you want it to grow healthy and strong, it needs more than just positive thoughts. It thrives on nourishing food, movement, and rest. Give it what it needs, and it will reward you with clarity, motivation, and momentum. Ignore those needs, and your mindset shifts may struggle to take root, just like a tree trying to grow in dry, depleted soil.

What you eat has a direct impact on your mood, your ability to focus, and your decision-making. Nutrient-dense foods support neurotransmitter production, which helps you feel more balanced and resilient. A handful of nuts, leafy greens, berries, and healthy fats might do more for your mindset than a fourth cup of coffee ever could.

MOVEMENT MATTERS

Physical activity stimulates dopamine, clears mental fog, and helps reset your nervous system. That doesn't mean you need to hit the gym like a pro athlete. A brisk walk, a little dancing in your kitchen, or even stretching between calls can make a noticeable difference in your energy and emotional resilience.

And then there's sleep. When you sleep, your brain literally cleans itself. It processes your emotions, locks in new habits, and resets your mental filters. If you've ever tried to make a confident decision on four hours of sleep, you already know how this works. The Bullshift journey is about clarity and intention. Sleep helps you get there.

This isn't about perfection. It's about giving your brain and body the support they need to help you show up for yourself and your goals. You're doing the inner work, but if your body's crashing, it's like trying to run a million-dollar business on two hours of sleep and a stale granola bar.

TIME TO PUT THAT ENERGY TO WORK!

Now that you're giving your brain the fuel it needs, it's time to build the internal tools that will keep your mindset strong and your thoughts working *for* you. In the next chapter, we'll explore simple but powerful ways to rewire your brain, starting with one of the most underestimated tools in the Bullshift toolbox: reframing. These shifts may seem subtle at first, but they create a ripple effect that transforms everything from your mood to your bank account.

CHAPTER 12

How to Develop a Growth Mindset and a Healthy Relationship with Money

"Change your thoughts, and you change your world."

– NORMAN VINCENT PEALE

By now, you've begun the powerful process of becoming more aware of your beliefs, especially the ones that have held you back around money and success. You've disrupted old thought patterns, challenged limiting stories, and practiced reframing them into something more supportive. This is amazing progress! Now it's time to explore how these mindset shifts can show up in your daily decisions and how they can begin to influence your financial results, business growth, and personal sense of freedom.

I once worked one-on-one with a group of female entrepreneurs who were part of an organization that supported, inspired, educated, and motivated women in business to grow from six to seven figures. American Express sponsored the organization and provided funds for 14 private coaching sessions for each member. Most of the ladies were generating revenues between $100,000 and $150,000 and had scalable business models in place. Most showed strong potential for growth.

I can confidently say that all these clients achieved many positive results from coaching, including increased confidence, improved business strategies, clearer understanding of their goals, and enhanced knowledge of how to make their business successful. However, of the 14 entrepreneurs I worked with, only eight continued coaching once American Express stopped providing the funds after their 12th session.

The entrepreneurs who didn't continue cited various reasons for dropping out of coaching, but most believed they couldn't afford to pay for it themselves. I was relatively new to being a coach at the time, so my fees were low. Too low! What was really going on behind the excuses these ladies made to deny themselves further support in achieving their success? What barriers kept these amazing women from exploring their fullest potential? I had a theory.

While most of the ladies in the group who stopped coaching believed they couldn't afford a continued coaching partnership, their limiting belief was rooted in a fear that ran much deeper than financial woes: Many had a strongly embedded belief that they would fail to achieve their one-million-dollar goal. They were afraid of failure.

As a coach, I knew that each of these entrepreneurs had a business model capable of reaching their one-million-dollar goal, but at that time in their lives, the business owners themselves could not embrace success. Their money trees were still just seeds, not receiving any nourishment in the form of confidence, energy, healthy beliefs, or actionable steps to grow into strong, abundant trees.

Today, I ask all the right questions of a coaching candidate to know if they're ready to grow their Money Tree and do the work to achieve success and financial freedom. A client's success is my success. As you continue to read this book and execute the Bullshift steps, I anticipate *your* success!

MINDSET MASTERY IS SIMPLE, BUT NOT ALWAYS EASY

I believe mindset mastery is *not* hard work—it's a commitment to simple steps that seem almost too easy to result in life-altering changes. You would think this insight would help more people to commit to consciously improving their mindset, but it can have quite the opposite effect.

People often shrug off these simple steps because of an engrained belief that anything worth achieving must be hard work, and they therefore believe these steps are too basic and too easy to create any worthwhile changes. They are wrong.

That said, a growth mindset can be fragile and requires daily devotion to maintain. You've got to fertilize, water, prune, and nurture your money tree! Some may think that's too difficult, but adding sustenance to your money tree can be engaging, even intriguing, when you make a game of it. Don't take yourself too seriously! If you make a mistake, forgive yourself and do a course correction. Learn from your mistake and store the lesson in your positive mindset database. You can do this! Go slow and expect results. Your expectation of progress will get your RAS buzzing with new information, reprogram your neural pathways, and support your vision of success!

In this next step, let's look at some habits and exercises you can use to incorporate positive mindset habits and practices into your daily routine.

CHANGE THE WAY YOU TALK ABOUT MONEY

Scientific studies show that positive and negative words don't only affect us on a deep psychological level, but they also significantly impact the outcomes of our entire lives. Both negative and positive self-talk affect our cognitive performance: studies show that positive self-talk is energizing and motivating, whereas negative self-talk leads to a decline in cognitive performance. The BS in your head can lead to anxiety, depression, social isolation, and even illness. A single word can influence the expression of genes that regulate physical and emotional stress in one direction or the other!

Positive words promote a healthy response in our brain and body, as well as in our reality. We all must teach ourselves to recognize our negative language and references, reframing them to achieve more positive results. Reframing is the process of consciously shifting the way you interpret a thought, belief, or situation so you can see it from a more empowering and constructive angle. It is not about pretending everything is fine when it is not. Instead, it is about choosing a perspective that supports growth and possibility.

Using supportive, positive language influences everything from your mood and emotions to your ability to recognize new opportunities. Reframing helps you break old thinking habits and replace them with new, more helpful ones. When you practice reframing often, you begin to rewire your brain. This means your brain builds new pathways for lasting change from the inside out. These pathways support calm, confidence, and clarity, even when life gets stressful.

> *"By holding a positive and optimistic [word] in your mind, you stimulate frontal lobe activity. This area includes specific language centers that connect directly to the motor cortex responsible for moving you into action. And as our research has shown, the longer you concentrate on positive words, the more you begin to affect other areas of the brain."*
>
> – ANDREW NEWBURG & MARK WALDMAN

COGNITIVE REFRAMING

One way to understand reframing your negative thoughts and words is to imagine looking through a camera lens. If you zoom in too closely, you might fixate on the flaws and miss the bigger picture. If you zoom out too far, you could overlook important details that matter. Reframing your thoughts is like adjusting the focus on that lens. A slight shift in how you view what's in front of you can completely change the image you see.

The essence of reframing is that your point of view shapes your experience. The frame through which you see a situation is built from your past experiences, memories, and beliefs. When you adjust that frame, even slightly, the meaning changes, and so does how you feel and respond.

You can reframe an entire situation or something as small as a single word or phrase. You'll be amazed at how quickly your perspective changes once you stop describing your financial situation in negative terms and start speaking about it with clarity and confidence.

Here are some examples of how you can reframe your money mindset and viewpoint by changing negative statements to positive statements.

Current	Reframe
"I never have enough money."	"I consistently meet my financial needs and am actively growing my wealth."
"I'll never succeed."	"I've seen some success and am building on it."
"You can't get rich without being a jerk."	"Plenty of nice people have money, and I intend to be one of them."

"I can't afford to hire help."	"I will get creative and find someone to help me with things at work and maybe at home."

The next Bullshift exercise will help you better familiarize yourself with the art of reframing.

Reframing isn't about pretending everything is perfect or forcing yourself to think positively all the time. It's about gently shifting your perspective so that you can move forward, instead of staying stuck in old stories.

Here are a few pointers before you dive in:

1. Start with Awareness, Not Judgment

If you catch yourself thinking something negative, that's actually a win. You're paying attention. Don't beat yourself up, just notice it, pause, and explore how else you might look at it.

2. Aim for Believability, Not Perfection

You don't have to go from "I'm terrible with money" to "I'm a billionaire genius." Find a statement that feels just a little bit better and more empowering than your original thought. Make it something your brain can accept. I imagine this process like taking one or two steps up a ladder, rather than trying to leap to the top.

3. Use Your Own Voice

Your reframe should sound like you, not like a motivational poster. Write it in a way that feels natural, grounded, and true to your personality. You're more likely to believe and repeat it often enough to make a difference.

4. Find the Evidence

If it's hard to believe your reframe, go back to the "evidence" you've captured about your successes and find one piece of evidence that supports your reframe. A past win, a compliment from a client, or progress you've made on a project, it all counts.

5. Practice Makes Powerful

Reframing is a muscle. The more you use it, the easier it becomes. At first, it might feel awkward; that's just your brain adjusting to a new, healthier path. Keep going!

BULLSHIFT EXERCISE 9

Now you give it a try! Use this space to jot down some of your negative statements about money, your ability to succeed, or anything else that fits into the realm of negative thinking. Then, translate them into supportive, positive messages:

Current	Reframe

Writing reframes can be tricky until you get the hang of it. Let's support this process with a simple but eye-opening experiment to show how much your words impact you, both emotionally and physically.

Look at the worksheet you just completed and choose one of your negative statements. Say it out loud, slowly and clearly. Pay close attention to how your body feels, how your energy shifts, and what emotions come up.

Example: "I will never have enough money."

Close your eyes and say that statement forcefully three times in a row. Then check in with your body: your shoulders, chest, stomach, neck, and head. How do you feel? Tense, upset, depressed? It does not send healthy messages to your body to say such things. How can you be positive and productive in this condition? You can't.

Now look at your positive reframe. Close your eyes and confidently say the statement.

Example: "I consistently meet my financial needs and am actively growing my wealth."

Check in with your body again. How do you feel? Better, right? Of course, you do! And from this feel-good place, you'll be far more innovative and productive. Your RAS will joyfully present more ideas and opportunities for you to achieve your next-step financial goals!

Even a slight shift in your physical or emotional state is a sign that your brain is responding. This is the power of language. The words you speak, especially the ones you say to yourself, influence your emotions, your confidence, and your results.

The more you use language that supports your growth, the easier it becomes to believe in your potential and act in alignment with your goals. Reframing isn't just mindset fluff; it is real, neurological work that rewires your brain for success.

Practice reframing daily by staying in tune with your body. It will tell you if your brain is feeding you BS that needs Bullshifting. When your mind and body are under excessive stress, you'll have headaches, tenseness, heartburn, high blood pressure, or almost any number of negative bodily sensations. Or, you may feel impatient, frustrated, or angry with those around you. When this happens, the odds are strong that your brain needs to reframe and reset. Living in a state of prolonged stress is unhealthy and stifling.

If your body is constantly signaling that something is off, don't ignore it. These symptoms are often more than just surface-level discomfort. They are red flags from your nervous system, warning you that stress has taken the wheel. To shift these patterns, we need to understand what's happening under the hood. That brings us to the very real and harmful impact of stress on your brain and body.

HOW STRESS HARMS US

Do you often struggle with high levels of anxiety? Or even worse, panic attacks? At its mildest, anxiety can be distracting and uncomfortable; at its worst, it can be mentally and physically crippling, leaving us feeling powerless and exposed. While there are ways to improve how we feel in these moments, anxiety can all too easily hijack the brain, making it easy to spiral deeper into negative thoughts, thus amplifying the fear and stress even more. Why does that happen?

We all want to feel protected from the anxiety-producing things that hurt us: painful remarks, unpleasant emotions, loss, and physical threats. Amazingly, our brains have a built-in sensor to support our quest for safety and protection: that tiny, almond-shaped part of the limbic system called the amygdala is best known for its role in fear processing. When exposed to fear-inducing stimuli, information about the situation is immediately communicated to the amygdala, which sends signals to the hypothalamus to trigger a "fight, flight, or freeze" response.

THE AMYGDALA AT WORK

Suppose you're back on your trail in the woods and you hear a creaking noise alerting you to a large tree limb about to fall right onto your path. Your eyes and ears will send the information to the amygdala, that area of the brain that contributes to emotional processing. The amygdala interprets the images and sounds. When it perceives danger, it instantly sends a distress signal to the hypothalamus. The hypothalamus is the brain's command center, communicating with the rest of the body through the nervous system so that you have the energy to fight or flee. Its fear-processing circuitry will instantly inform the pituitary gland and adrenals to react to this life-threatening situation. Those organs, in turn, will release adrenaline and cortisol (both are hormones) into the bloodstream. The resulting increase in oxygen and metabolism gives your muscles the boost they need for you to flee or fight and remove yourself (or someone else) from the path of danger. In short, your brain assesses danger instantly and yells down to the other organs to give you a nearly superhuman boost of energy.

My daughter once experienced the most remarkable effects of this process at work. She tragically witnessed someone trapped under the weight of an 800-pound piece of forestry equipment. Without giving it a thought, she found the strength to lift the heavy object off the victim, allowing enough clearance for another party to drag him out from under the nearly half-ton object. Sadly, it was too late for the victim. Had my daughter stopped to assess the situation, she would have known this, but the effects of adrenaline and cortisol had hijacked her brain and boosted her body into action.

Stories like this are examples of the amygdala and other brain parts communicating to provide the energy we need to act in extreme situations, such as when we need to save a life. To me, this natural process is nothing short of astonishing, but it does have a dark side.

THE DOUBLE-EDGED SWORD OF THE AMYGDALA

On a good day, you might wake up, get dressed, and step outside to be greeted by a lovely sunny morning. Hopefully, you take a moment to appreciate the day's possibilities. I enjoy walking out onto my deck to enjoy the sounds and sights of my beautiful koi pond. These moments always bring an easy smile to my face, joy to my heart, and set the pace for a pleasant day.

For most of us, regardless of our particular routine, each morning offers the freedom to choose our activities from the safety of our homes. We often forget what a privilege these choices and experiences are for us.

But now allow your imagination to travel back in time to the Paleolithic period, about 2.5 million years ago. Back then, early humans lived in caves or simple dwellings. Our caveman ancestors spent their days hunting for food and defending themselves against the physical threat of predators. They did not enjoy the privilege of stepping into the sunshine to anticipate a safe, pleasant day. They did not know for sure that there would be food to nourish them. No, they were too busy being on the lookout and defending themselves against threats of attack by mastodons, saber-toothed tigers, cave lions, woolly rhinoceroses, and more. The fight, flight, or freeze instincts of the brain's limbic system gave them the best chances of remaining alive. In short, the amygdala was hard at work 24/7, protecting early humans from genuinely life-threatening situations.

Over time, the powerful processing system in our brains has followed evolution's lead, lowering the threshold of what it considers a threat. Since we no longer face such high daily risks, our caveman brain (or our primal brain) finds other "dangers" to warn us about. Now, everyday problems can trigger an anxious individual's fight, flight, or freeze responses. Our primitive ancestors didn't have the luxury of worrying about their children's future. (Well, except whether they would survive the day.) They could not step away from the demands of their protective instincts to obsess about what others might think of them, whether they would be on the receiving end of hurtful remarks, or if they were going to experience relationship, financial, or work stress—things that now cause daily pressure in fretful minds.

Most of these perceived dangers originate within us, in the form of worry and dread, rather than from an external force that might cause us physical harm. Most of our fear comes from . . . well, the fear of fear! Our brains are programmed toward having a negative bias, making it challenging to find peace and happiness. The human mind was not created to be positive because it had to survive. It had to be skeptical and alert. Negative thoughts travel faster and are stickier than positive ones, making it more natural to let our beliefs flow into a river of negativity unconstructively. Our brain simply hasn't adapted since society's transition from pure survival to the goal of being happy most of the time.

This is where your Bullshift exercises come in! Engaging in mindset work like Bullshifting to challenge and change negative belief systems can help reduce fearful or negative thinking, making your amygdala less reactive. When you consistently work to shift your mindset away from fear-based thinking, it can reduce the amygdala's tendency to trigger stress and fear-based responses. This concept is supported by research in neuroscience, which has shown that practices like cognitive restructuring, mindfulness, and other positive psychology techniques can decrease amygdala reactivity over time.

Doing the essential inner work laid out in this book can have a calming effect on the amygdala and lead to more balanced emotional responses. Your stress will be reduced significantly! Your days will go from a blur of unproductive activities such as putting out fires at work, flitting from task to task, feeling bogged down with BS thoughts, to being able to implement clear and concise action steps.

This shift in mindset not only calms your stress response but also directly impacts how you approach your daily tasks. When you're no longer consumed by fear or negative thoughts, you can focus more clearly and take intentional and practical steps forward. In turn, your productivity will naturally increase.

PRODUCTIVITY DECLINES WITH STRESS

I know your days are busy, but are those hours productive? Anxiety-inducing thoughts will exponentially decrease your productivity! That's another reason to employ your reframing techniques. Financial stress is a big productivity sucker. If your thoughts cause stress to the degree of initiating anxiety or even panic, your brain will be unable to function anywhere near capacity, and you'll be reactive instead of responsive. That's when significant, time-consuming, and costly mistakes are made.

Did you know you cannot focus, think, or problem-solve when you go into a fight, flight, or freeze response? The steroid hormones triggered during this response (adrenaline and cortisol) help us cope with and prepare for survival-based actions. If your thoughts create a sense of false danger and fast action is actually *un*necessary, you won't use up the adrenaline and cortisol, and your body will be left feeling anxious.

When stress becomes significant to the point of inducing anxiety, about 80% of the blood that should go to our brain is redirected to our extremities instead. We are not designed to *think* our way out of an emergency; we are designed to fight, flee, or freeze during an emergency, and our brains interpret anxiety as an emergency. When high stress or severe anxiety sets in and we feel foggy and indecisive, the loss of blood to the brain is one of the reasons why. So, let's keep the blood flowing to that brain!

PUT YOUR BULLSHIFT TOOLS TO WORK

The next time anxiety, frustration, a sense of being overwhelmed, and/or brain fog set in, let it serve as a reminder to use what you are learning in this book! You can begin by *reducing your anxiety with controlled breathing.*

While it can be challenging to control our breathing when we're in an anxious state, deep breathing is imperative. Your body will not sustain a severe panic attack or elevated levels of anxiety while it's receiving measured, yet high levels of cleansing oxygen from deep breathing. Breathing signals the nervous system to calm down, so take long, deep breaths, inhaling through your nose, expanding your abdomen, and releasing your breath through your mouth. Then utilize these strategies:

- Identify if your negative thoughts are false, partially true, or really, really true. Shift the BS to a realistic viewpoint of your situation and its consequences.
- Use the reframing technique to reframe your thoughts to something more positive and hopeful.
- Create an intention to release your stress and feel peace while you're doing your deep breathing. *"I intend to be at peace as I release this stress."*
- Use powerful affirmations and words instead of negative, deflating language.
- Put a little vacation into each and every day.

And don't forget to ask for help! That's something entrepreneurs aren't especially good at. Help could be in the form of assistance at work, someone to process your thoughts with, someone to assist with responsibilities at home and with the kids, or whatever else would ease your burden at the time.

Remember, asking for help is not a sign of weakness; it's a sign of strength. If you ever hesitate to reach out, try reversing the roles. How would you feel if someone you cared about kept silently struggling instead of asking you for support? Chances are, you'd want them to lean on you. So, give your loved ones, friends, or employees that same opportunity. When you avoid asking for help, you're not only denying yourself support, but you're also denying them the chance to show up for you. Let the people in your life feel like superheroes by helping the one they think never needs saving—you!

OWN THE SHIFT

Reframing your thoughts, interrupting old belief loops, and reducing stress are not just feel-good strategies. They begin the process of rewiring your brain. Every time you challenge a limiting belief, you weaken an old neural pathway, and each time you practice a healthier thought, you strengthen a new one. This is how a stronger mindset and a healthier relationship with money take root. But lasting change does not come from thinking differently alone. It also requires feeling differently.

Your emotional state shapes your behavior, your decisions, and the opportunities you are able to notice. If you use positive words but still carry doubt, fear, or tension in your body, your brain will stay stuck in survival mode. It will block progress and push away possibility. In the next chapter, we will deepen your transformation by aligning your thoughts and emotions so you can generate and embody the energy that attracts clarity, confidence, and financial growth.

CHAPTER 13
Be the Energy You Want to Attract

Talk of energy is not woo-woo. Energy is not a mystical force or a fluffy personal development idea. Energy is communication. It is real and observable in the way you think, speak, move, and respond to life. Before you say a single word, people can feel your energy. They sense whether you are confident or uncertain, open or guarded, grounded or chaotic. Your energy speaks for you, and it either pulls opportunities toward you or pushes them away. That is why mindset alone is not enough. You also benefit from managing your energy with the same level of intention.

Energy is not created by accident. It is shaped by your thoughts, your self-belief, your nervous system, and your emotional state. You carry it into every conversation, every client interaction, every pitch, every decision. When your energy is calm, focused, and self-assured, you make better decisions, build stronger relationships, and notice more opportunities. When your energy is tense, scattered, or doubtful, success starts to feel like a struggle rather than a natural outcome. You have already learned how thoughts shape your reality. Now it is time to understand how energy works in the same way.

LIKE ATTRACTS LIKE

The energy you bring into a room, whether calm and confident or anxious and scattered, affects your tone, posture, facial expressions, and even the words you choose. People pick up on those signals and respond to them, often without being consciously aware of it. That is why your energy is not invisible and is magnetic by nature.

Imagine you are in a team brainstorming session. The room is lively, and ideas are flowing. Then Alex speaks up. He is excited, curious, and fully engaged. His enthusiasm fuels the conversation, and everyone becomes more creative and willing to contribute. One person's energy elevates the entire room.

Now picture the same meeting, but instead of Alex, Mark walks in, looking frustrated and distracted. With a heavy sigh, he drops into his chair and declares, "No, that's not going to work." The air shifts. People hesitate. The group becomes guarded. Momentum disappears. A few people try to regain the flow, but Mark's negative energy lingers, and the whole team feels stuck. Mark never said he wanted to shut down collaboration, yet his energy did it for him.

This isn't just a meeting dynamic; it can happen anywhere. Your energy influences how people respond to you, whether they trust you, and whether they want to work with you, refer you, or buy from you. Your energy affects whether doors open or quietly close.

INTERNAL SIGNALS CREATE EXTERNAL RESULTS

Your energy is shaped by what is happening inside you. Every thought carries an emotional charge, and that charge affects your mood, decisions, and behavior. Your thoughts and energy work together to either move you forward or keep you stuck in cycles of stress, doubt, and scarcity.

This is where the Reticular Activating System (RAS) comes in. As you learned earlier, the RAS acts as your brain's filter. It decides what information gets your attention based on what you focus on most. If your thoughts are rooted in fear or scarcity, your RAS will highlight more struggle, more hesitation, and more so-called proof that things will not work out. You will unintentionally filter your world through limitation.

But when your energy shifts, your focus shifts. When you practice gratitude, reframe your thoughts, and choose possibility, your emotional state changes, and your RAS follows your lead. Suddenly, you begin to notice people who can help you, solutions you did not see before, and opportunities that were already available to you. You simply were not aligned with them yet.

ENERGY IS CONTAGIOUS

Energy is contagious. When you consistently show up with optimism, confidence, and a sense of possibility, that ripple spreads through your clients, your team, your family, and your community. It is an energy that keeps on giving. When your thoughts, emotions, and energy are aligned, you experience momentum with less resistance. You stop chasing outcomes and begin attracting them. This is especially important in leadership.

As a leader, you are influential, and nothing influences people faster than energy. Your team will mirror the emotional tone you bring into a room. If you are calm, they feel grounded. If you are overwhelmed, they feel pressured. If you carry doubt, they hesitate. If you show up with conviction and clarity, they rise with you. Words matter, but energy **amplifies** the message. When your energy and intentions align, people follow with enthusiasm.

This is why your energy is vital to the growth of your money tree. You cannot build a successful business with misaligned energy. You might push your way to results for a while, but it will be exhausting and unsustainable. Growth rooted in stress eventually collapses. Growth rooted in grounded, intentional energy becomes unstoppable.

To stay aligned, combine the Bullshift insights from this book with a simple daily routine. That might include ten minutes of morning journaling, a midday walk, and a short gratitude practice before bed. These habits reinforce your mindset shifts and help you stay grounded, focused, and receptive. When you tend to your inner world consistently, your outer world begins to shift with it. **Mindset mastery begins with awareness and intentionality.**

Start by examining your current energy. What are you broadcasting to the world? If you lead with stress, frustration, or doubt, you will continue to magnetize those same conditions. Shift your energy by committing to daily practices that support emotional alignment. Bullshift exercises, meditation, yoga, visualization, and affirmations are powerful tools to support this work. Surround yourself with people, environments, and routines that expand your energy and support your growth.

You are the creator of your reality, and your energy is the blueprint.

SETTING GOALS IS POWERFUL—SETTING INTENTIONS WILL GET YOU WHAT YOU WANT

Your energy blueprint is like a muscle. It requires attention and consistency to stay strong. Setting intentions is one of the most effective ways to align your actions with the energy you want to bring into your life. I am not talking about setting goals. Entrepreneurs already understand the value of setting goals, but few truly understand the power of setting intentions.

You may be wondering, what is the difference?

Goal setting helps you clarify what you want, create a plan, and stay focused on a future result. That is valuable, but there is a downside. Goals pull your focus into the future and emphasize what you have not yet achieved. If you do not hit a goal, you may begin carrying the emotional weight of disappointment or even shame. When that happens, your energy shifts into scarcity, frustration, or pressure, and that energy works against you. You do not want to carry the emotional baggage of failure while you are building the life and business you desire. That negative energy will stunt the growth of your money tree. This is where intentions become powerful.

HOW SETTING INTENTIONS WILL INFLUENCE YOUR ENERGY TO ATTRACT WEALTH

Setting intentions helps you get out of your head and focus on what matters in the moment. Whether you are preparing for a crucial meeting or starting your day, intentions direct your attention away from distractions and toward meaningful action. Speaking your intentions out loud helps shift your energy from worry to purpose. It also interrupts negative thought patterns, helping you focus on solutions rather than problems.

When you clearly define your immediate goals and intentions, you become more aware of your choices. This awareness increases your ability to follow through, make aligned decisions, and create consistent progress. Research shows that individuals who set both goals and intentions are more likely to take meaningful action, follow through on commitments, and make strategic financial decisions. Intention keeps your mindset aligned so you can fuel your success with energy, not force.

SETTING INTENTIONS WILL CHANGE HOW YOU EXPERIENCE LIFE

Have you ever attended a networking event filled with people who are desperately handing out business cards? You know the type. They are not present, not listening, and not interested in connection. Their only goal is to close a sale. They have no idea how powerful intention is, so they operate from a place of fear and scarcity. They are focused on transactions, not relationships, and their energy repels the very opportunities they are chasing.

When I attend an event, write articles, work on this book, or speak to an audience, I begin with a simple intention:

"I intend to be my authentic self, help those I connect with feel heard and valued, and have a meaningful impact on at least one person in the room (or one reader)."

What happens when I do this? My energy shifts. I feel relaxed, aligned, and comfortable being myself. I am not trying to impress anyone or prove anything. I am focused on connection. As a result, I naturally attract people who share similar values and beliefs. Conversations become enjoyable, meaningful, and effortless. Real opportunities grow from these relationships because they are built on trust and respect, not pressure.

Stating your intention before entering a situation increases your self-awareness and helps you show up as your best self. It also takes the pressure off. When your purpose is clear, you do not need to force anything. You simply show up as yourself and allow the right people and outcomes to connect with you.

ACHIEVE YOUR GOALS WHEN YOU SET INTENTIONS ALONGSIDE THE GOALS

When you set a goal like increasing your company's revenue by 15% by the end of the third quarter, you have created a measurable objective. That is a strong start, but a financial target alone will not get you there. You need clear steps, structure, and commitment. This is where many entrepreneurs struggle. They set the goal, but they do not create the system or the consistency needed to achieve it.

Let's say part of your revenue plan includes improving your local search ranking on Google. You decide that one way to do this is to collect five-star customer reviews. It is a solid and measurable plan.

You add it to your to-do list and feel good about it. Then another day goes by. Then another week. Suddenly, it has been two months, and nothing has changed. You had a worthwhile goal, but you did not create the follow-through. Why? You never set the intention behind the goal.

When you set a clear intention, your energy shifts. You take ownership of the process and make room for disciplined action. For example:

"I intend to spend the next two hours creating a system to collect Google reviews from our customers. I will silence my phone, pause email, and focus fully on this task. This new procedure will be complete by 2 p.m., and I will complete the process with ease and clarity."

When you speak your intention, you raise your energy, engage your mind, nervous system, and subconscious all at once. You tell your brain what to focus on, how long to focus, and why it matters. This level of clarity reduces procrastination and increases follow-through. You are no longer interested in the goal conceptually. You are committed to taking action.

INTENTIONS AREN'T ONLY FOR WORK-RELATED ACTIVITIES

Intentions are not just for business goals and productivity. They can transform your personal life as well.

For example, when I get behind the wheel of my car, I often set a simple intention before I drive:

"I intend to get to and from my destination safely and without incident. Thank you, Universe."

This intention reminds me to stay calm and calls me back if I am not focused on my driving. It keeps me present and aware, not rushed or distracted.

Family and personal time benefit from intentions too. How often do you sit with someone you love while your mind drifts back to work, unfinished tasks, or worries? You may physically be there, but emotionally, you are somewhere else. Setting an intention helps you choose how you want to experience a moment. For example:

"I intend to enjoy this time with my family. I intend to be present, relaxed, and grateful in this moment."

When you set a simple intention like this, you give your nervous system a command. You choose peace over pressure. You honor what really matters in life. You become the kind of person who is not just successful but fulfilled.

SET POWERFUL INTENTIONS NOW

Allow me to suggest that, for the next week, you begin setting daily intentions and tracking the outcomes. This practice will help you develop focus, confidence, emotional clarity, and consistency. Intentions keep you connected to what matters and shift your energy before you take action.

Think about opportunities or activities that occur frequently in your life. These might include team meetings, sales calls, difficult conversations, project work, family time, workouts, or even your morning routine. Each of these moments will benefit from setting a clear intention before you begin.

Below is an example to get you started.

Opportunity or Activity: Talking to a prospect.

Most people enter a prospect meeting with one thing on their mind: closing the sale. That is the wrong approach. I am not offering full-blown sales advice here, but I can tell you that success has little to do with chasing the sale and everything to do with building trust. When your intention is solely to close, your energy becomes pressured, and people can sense it. However, when you intend to serve, connect, and understand, your energy shifts—and so does the outcome.

Your True Intention: To help the prospect.

"I intend to listen carefully to their needs and concerns and establish a meaningful and mutual foundation of trust. I intend to acknowledge and validate this person, offer honesty, clarity, and kindness, and help them in any reasonable way I can."

This intention has created powerful results in my business. Before I speak with a prospective coaching client, I set a caring intention. It is never about getting the sale. It is about truly hearing and helping the person in front of me. My close rate is about 80%. Why? Because intention builds trust, and trust builds business.

BULLSHIFT EXERCISE 10

Now it's your turn. Use these pages for the next week or so. Identify at least one opportunity (like an important conversation or meeting) and/or one activity per day, then set your intention for each one. At the end of the day, take a few notes on your outcome. Did you feel more focused and less pressured? Did you complete a task or experience a different result than usual?

Today's Date: ______________________________

Opportunity or Activity:

____

____

____

____

____

Intention:

____

____

____

____

____

Outcome:

____

____

____

____

____

Notes and Observations:

____

____

____

____

____

Energy and intention shape your reality, but belief fuels it. When you align your thoughts and actions with clear intentions, you begin to move through life with purpose instead of pressure. You no longer chase results. You create them. But to truly attract what you desire, you must believe you are worthy of receiving it. That is the next step in your Bullshift journey. In the following chapter, we will explore the foundation of true success: believing in your value and owning your worth with confidence.

CHAPTER 14
Believe in Your Value!

Service-based business owners are sometimes guilty of a very misled belief when it comes to value—I know I was! It often comes from the assumption that, since we're here to help people, reducing our rates is okay, even expected! We may even offer to help someone for free. Whether you're a coach, designer, accountant, or in the healing arts, your passion is likely about helping people live a better life. But what about you? Don't *you* deserve an equally satisfying life?

Here is where many people struggle to recognize their own value. When something comes naturally to you, it is easy to minimize it or assume everyone can do what you do. That is rarely true. Think about coaches, therapists, consultants, teachers, or anyone who helps people grow. A great coach does not recite formulas. A great coach draws from experience, intuition, compassion, and a natural ability to see what others cannot. When I first began coaching, I often wondered where my insights came from. I would hear myself say something that landed so clearly for a client that even I paused for a moment. Clients would ask, "How did you know exactly what I needed to hear?" or "You make it seem so simple. Why did I not see that?" The reality is, we all have gifts that feel effortless to us, but powerful to others. Never underestimate your gifts and talents!

When something feels natural or easy, putting a price tag on it is *not* easy. People who are quite empathic may feel greedy and wrong to charge much money for their services. Some struggle with charging any money at all! But remember, what may come naturally and easy to you is likely inaccessible to others.

For instance, instead of coaching someone at a very low rate because it doesn't feel like a lot of work, look at the outcome the client experiences, rather than the amount of effort you put into the session. A natural gift doesn't always take effort. Base your fees on the results you generate for others, not the work you do. Of course, if you're, say, an accountant, your fees are based on output and time, but again, even if your job feels manageable, that should *not* equate to charging low prices for your service. Keep your rates competitive and don't strive to be the cheapest accountant on the block!

DETERMINE YOUR RATES AND STAND BY THEM

When I was in the "lack of self-value" loop after I had lost all my money, I had to work long hours to pay my bills. I kept my coaching rates "affordable." The misguided reasoning I applied was that the people I loved to work with couldn't afford more for a coach, but the truth was that I didn't believe in myself, nor did I place a high value on my work and the results seen by my clients. My money mindset had improved somewhat since my devastating financial loss, but it still needed much work. I could keep our home and purchase the necessities, but I still struggled and there was no room in the budget for non-necessities.

I was helping others attract business, increase revenues, and break free from the confines of their negative thoughts and circumstances. Why was I not doing a better job of that myself? I didn't criticize myself (much) because I had come a long way. I was making more money than most coaches, but my income was far from what was necessary to support my family and live without financial stress. I was stuck and I knew it. Again, the Universe intervened by sending another eye-opening experience my way.

IF YOU DON'T HAVE ENOUGH BUSINESS, IT'S NOT BECAUSE YOUR RATES ARE TOO HIGH

It was during this time of struggle that I acted on a coaching inquiry that had come through my website from a woman whom I viewed as being my perfect client. After our phone conversation, she was ready to sign the contract and pay for the first month of coaching for her and her business partner. After verbally agreeing to become a client, she said, "Oh, I guess I should ask about your rates." It was an afterthought, which meant she could afford a good coach.

When I proudly announced my pathetically low rate, she was surprised and hesitant. After only a moment, she stated that I wasn't the coach for her and said goodbye. She had clearly anticipated much higher fees from a coach with my background and experience and then had decided she'd made an error in judgment. How could I be a good coach if I charged so little?

Lesson learned. That experience was just what I needed to stop telling myself BS stories about what people could afford. I asked myself, "Do you want to attract clients who can afford you and want to work toward their goals successfully, or do you want to attract people who engage in a poverty mindset and are unwilling to pay you what you're worth?"

If you have a mindset similar to mine before I restructured my business model, start by researching competitive rates in your field. Use the worksheet below to take notes. Then list examples of the outcomes or results you deliver to your clients. What does it mean to your clients when they achieve these goals? Can you even put a price tag on them?

Lastly, create a new model! Remember, it's not just *what* you charge for your service, it's *how* you charge. For instance, when I changed my business model, I not only increased my pricing but went from monthly billing to a lump sum annual billing. Charging up front for a year of coaching gives me financial stability, creates a stronger bond between me and my clients, and garners better results for my clients because they are more committed to the process.

Also consider opportunities for upselling and add-ons.

BULLSHIFT EXERCISE 11

List three competitors that are successful:

1. ______________________________
2. ______________________________
3. ______________________________

Next, find out what they charge for similar services. I've actually called coaches and asked! You'd be surprised at how helpful some people are. List their rates here:

1. ______________________________
2. ______________________________
3. ______________________________

What did you learn about pricing? Is their model different than yours? Do they sell services or merchandise that you don't sell? List those differences here:

____

____

____

____

____

What else do your competitors do differently?

What outcomes do they offer?

What are the outcomes for *your* clients? List all you can think of.

What does it mean to your clients when they achieve their goals?

What are the options for your new pricing model? i.e., higher prices, more frequent billing, creating product or service bundles, etc.

How much will you charge for what number or length of services?

____

____

____

____

____

(*Note:* My previously too-low fee included four sessions a month. When I raised my prices and changed my model, I dropped that to three monthly sessions.)

Fill in your new intentions:

My total gross profit [before expenses] for the last four quarters was:

____.

With my new pricing model, additional marketing, and my new money mindset in place, I stand to increase my gross profit over the next __________________ by __________________ [dollar amount or percentage].

ACCOUNTABILITY AND TIMETABLES

Don't forget to give yourself a timetable for your changes and goals! Back when I did my daily ritual to find clarity on my business model, all I did was change my mind and write down my new process, so it took no time at all.

If you record significant differences between your company and companies like yours and you want to change your marketing, first define your goals and deadline dates to create accountability for yourself. However, do *not* use these changes as an excuse to delay your pricing structure! (When I changed my model, I didn't change my website or marketing language, only my contract. The marketing came later.) Remember, once you erase your BS and find clarity, you *will* attract more of what you want. Mindset work is a vital part of your marketing efforts!

When you truly tap into the power of your visualizations, you'll find yourself inspired to practice the technique regularly. I still practice client-attraction visualization whenever I have openings in my schedule: I vividly imagine a new prospect's energy and a vague image of their face, and then I open my heart to welcome them in, feeling the excitement of knowing I can help transform their life and business profoundly. I often say that this type of visualization is my secret marketing weapon because it works like magic!

DO YOU DESERVE TO BE SUCCESSFUL AND WEALTHY?

Do you remember my client Jason who inherited his parents' estate and questioned whether he deserved that wealth? He's not alone in his doubts. Many entrepreneurs struggle with feelings of worthiness and deserving. This often leads to subconscious self-sabotage. From my coaching experience, I've learned to recognize common signs when clients are holding themselves back. While there are many symptoms, two especially stand out: downplaying achievements and lacking confidence around their worth and value.

When someone questions their value and worthiness, they may downplay their success. In my earlier life, I also had this issue. It stemmed from childhood, of course, and fortunately, I learned to redefine my self-worth and left those unhealthy tendencies behind long ago.

It took me a while to overcome my own value-questioning, though. When I worked at NBC, I was part of a team that won a National Emmy Award. That was no small achievement, yet I told no one! Not my husband, my mother, or my best friend. It wasn't until years later that I realized the reason for my secrecy: I felt like an imposter! I believed I hadn't done anything special enough to deserve such a great honor.

When I let it slip that the team I was on had won this prestigious award, my good friend Ruth helped me identify my misguided logic. She demanded to know why I'd never shared this remarkable achievement with her for all those years. I believed I could justify my thinking to her since it made perfect sense—to me, anyway. You see, I was a part of a team, so the National Emmy would have been awarded to the station even if I hadn't been involved. Although the award-winning campaign was partly my idea, and I had helped execute many of the pieces, I told myself that the team would have won the award without me. My contributions were not critical to the campaign's success. Or at least, that's what I told myself. "Everyone else deserved the award, but not you!" my inner voice kept saying. I believed those lies at the deepest levels of my psyche.

And that kind of false narrative didn't end with the National Emmy Award experience. I applied my misguided logic to much of what I did. Notice the half-truths in the following statements! By the time I was 25, I had a significant amount of money in fruitful investments, but that was just dumb luck. It took only a few years after being out of school before I earned more than most people in similar jobs did many years into their careers, but I was just in the right place at the right time. It had nothing to do with skill and value, I told myself.

I didn't know it then, but I had a solid case of what I would soon identify as imposter syndrome.

DO YOU HAVE FEELINGS OF BEING AN IMPOSTER?

Imposter syndrome is the belief that you are not as capable or qualified as others think you are, even when you have clear evidence of success (which you are collecting now!). Many entrepreneurs experience it because they are constantly learning as they go and there is no formal structure to validate their progress. Running a business requires making decisions without guarantees, which can create self-doubt and a fear of being exposed as inexperienced.

Entrepreneurs also tend to compare themselves to others, overlook their own wins, and assume their strengths are nothing special because they come naturally. Imposter syndrome is not a lack of ability. It is a habit of doubting your own value, which is total BS!

Here are only a few of the many signs indicating that you too may suffer from this malady of the mind and spirit:

1. You sometimes feel like a fraud.

Do you ever fear that others will discover you're not as competent or knowledgeable as you seem? Even with external validation, you might worry about being "exposed" or "found out," feeling like you don't truly deserve the success you've achieved. When the team at NBC won the Emmy Award, my first thought was that they were being kind to me by including my name on the award. *I certainly did nothing to deserve it,* I thought. I actually felt embarrassed to have been included!

2. You downplay achievements.

Is it difficult for you to accept a compliment? When others acknowledge your success, do you downplay it, attributing it to luck or external factors instead of your hard work or talent? Those who carry the burden of imposter syndrome beliefs may feel like they landed in the right place at the right time and simultaneously had a stroke of luck. Or one stroke of luck after another.

3. You minimize your success.

Do you have difficulty celebrating milestones, often thinking your achievements aren't significant or don't count? People with imposter syndrome often feel like they're "faking it" and fear they'll be exposed as frauds. This mindset prevents them from fully embracing their achievements or feeling like they deserve greater success and wealth.

If you recognize imposter syndrome behaviors as a part of your own psychology, the Bullshift exercises are a great place to begin your transformation! Just as I was, you may be entirely convinced by the so-called "logic" that explains away your success, but that's faulty thinking. By looking for the truth instead of the lies you tell yourself, reframing your negative statements, and identifying your actual value, you'll plant your feet firmly on the path to happiness and success.

But imposter syndrome is not the only self-sabotaging behavior that diminishes happiness and reward. I see people struggle to believe they deserve success and wealth due to psychological, social, and cultural factors. We've covered many of these self-limiting patterns in previous chapters, but let's take a second look at some of them.

4. You have limiting beliefs.

Many people develop limiting beliefs early in life, often rooted in their upbringing or past experiences. Messages like "money is the root of all evil" or "success comes with sacrifices" or "rich people are greedy" can create internal barriers. These beliefs can lead to feelings of guilt or unworthiness when pursuing success or wealth, so success is hard to come by, or has a self-imposed threshold.

5. You feel fear of failure (or success).

Yes, it's true! Many entrepreneurs fear that success will bring pressure, responsibility, or expectations they feel unequipped to handle. This fear creates a mental block, convincing them that they're better off avoiding success altogether. This in turn leads to self-sabotage or underachievement.

Entrepreneurs who shoulder the entire burden of their day-to-day business naturally feel overwhelmed and out of balance. The thought of growth is petrifying and immobilizing! Additional work indeed comes with growth, but if you learn to scale your business correctly, you'll lower your stress rather than increase it.

6. Your childhood conditioning continues to affect you.

What we learn about money and success during childhood can profoundly impact our beliefs. If you recall in my childhood story, my brain was programmed to believe there's always just enough money to get by, but never more. In an earlier BS exercise, you examined your own money mindset related childhood beliefs and where they came from. Now, re-examine how those beliefs could be contributing to your own version of The Imposter Syndrome.

If you grew up in an environment where money was scarce or you were taught that being "too successful" was arrogant or selfish, you may carry these narratives into adulthood, making it hard to believe that you deserve wealth.

7. Societal and cultural messages impact your beliefs.

Society often sends mixed messages about success and wealth. In some cultures, or communities, pursuing wealth may be seen as materialistic or shallow, creating inner conflict. People may feel guilty about wanting more than what's deemed "acceptable" by their family, culture, or social group.

8. You fear being judged.

The fear of being judged by others for success or wealth can lead entrepreneurs to downplay their ambitions. They may worry that their peers or loved ones will see them as greedy, superficial, or unrelatable, which can cause them to distance themselves from the idea of wealth.

9. Past failures haunt you.

This is a big one for entrepreneurs. If they've faced significant challenges like a failed business, they might internalize those experiences as proof that they do not deserve or are incapable of future success.

10. You need to break out of your comfort zone.

Many people have a subconscious "set point" regarding success and wealth. Based on their background, this is the level of achievement or financial security they're comfortable with. Anything beyond that can feel threatening or unfamiliar, leading to discomfort and self-sabotage when trying to achieve more. Make sure to do the Bullshift exercises in this book to identify and stretch your comfort zone!

11. You have success guilt.

In some cases, people feel guilty about achieving success or wealth when others around them are struggling. This is particularly common among people from less-affluent backgrounds or communities. They might downplay their success or feel undeserving because they don't want to leave others behind.

Breaking free from all these struggles involves raising your awareness of limiting beliefs, challenging those beliefs, and gradually replacing them with empowering thoughts, just as you've been doing as you've been reading this book. Understanding that success and wealth are not inherently "bad" or "undeserved" is a crucial first step toward allowing yourself to experience abundance and achieve your goals.

Don't stunt the growth of your money tree by holding on to a single one of these debilitating beliefs!

You were not meant to doubt yourself or apologize for your success. You were meant to grow, to contribute, and to experience the rewards of your gifts. Your money tree cannot thrive if you question your own value or shrink to make others comfortable. Owning your worth is not ego. It is emotional responsibility and a commitment to your future. When you believe in your value, you create the foundation for financial growth. In the next chapter, we will build on that foundation by turning belief into action. You will set clear income intentions and use a powerful gratitude practice to expand your wealth with purpose and confidence.

CHAPTER 15

Setting Intentions to Grow Your Money Tree

You now understand the power of believing in your value. When you own your worth, you open the door to receiving more of what you want. It is time to invite abundance! In this chapter, we will shift from mindset into measurable growth by setting financial intentions for your business (this can be done for your personal finances too!). Hopefully, you have been using your mindset mastery tools daily, because every reframe and every intention you set strengthens the health and abundance of your money tree.

Now we will focus on growing your income with purpose, beginning with one of the most important commitments you will ever make as an entrepreneur: paying yourself well and with confidence.

PAYING YOURSELF IS A MINDSET DECISION

Too often, I speak with business owners who "just take what is left over at the end of the month" as a paycheck. This is not a good practice. You are a priority in your business. Your money tree will never achieve abundance if you put your financial needs last. You need and deserve a regular paycheck. Neglecting to pay yourself builds a money mindset rooted in scarcity. Talk to your accountant about setting up proper payroll, even if you do not have employees. With automatic deductions and a consistent paycheck, your business will feel more legitimate, and so will you. More importantly, paying yourself is a powerful step in erasing the effects of imposter thinking, and claiming your value as a business owner.

Think about your future self. No matter where you live in the world, it is important to plan for long-term financial security. Talk with a qualified financial advisor in your country about contributing to a retirement plan and setting up proper tax and social benefits deductions. The sooner you begin, the stronger and more secure your financial future will be.

But how do I issue myself a regular paycheck if I don't have predictable cash flow?

The answer is simple: you *intend* to have a more predictable cash flow! Remember earlier in the book when I said mindset work is simple but not always easy? Sometimes the most challenging part is believing in yourself and the power of your mind.

The topic of money truly tests the entrepreneur. Let's use your Bullshift tools to rewire your brain so that you view your access to money as a natural process instead of an impossible struggle. The first thing you need to do is believe with *all* your heart and mind that money is here for you. Now! Today! Practice your visualization and reframe your negative statements. (Remember to watch out for those partly true, partly false statements.) Create your vision board. Go all out! And remember, your brain, including your RAS, cannot differentiate between something that is vividly imagined and actual reality. Make your new income goal a reality before it even happens!

YOUR REALISTIC MAGIC WAND

It's now time to break out what I call a *realistic magic wand.* "Magic" because it helps the brain stretch beyond its comfort zone.

"Realistic" because if you took home $25,000 last year and you shoot for $1,000,000 this year, you may be setting yourself up to fail.

When setting growth goals, intentions are meant to create commitment, clarity, and focus. They should be realistic but also outside of your comfort zone. Do everything you can to suspend the belief that you cannot make more money. Be playful and curious instead! What if you *did* make more money? Tap into the power of limitless possibilities! Don't think about *how* you'll make your new money goal happen, believe that you *will* make it happen. Thus, the reason for your realistic magic wand as you complete this next Bullshift exercise.

BULLSHIFT EXERCISE 12

When you set your income number, go big enough to feel uncomfortable, yet allow yourself to be excited about it. Make it seem just out of reach, but also make it realistically match your potential for earnings.

My personal income for the past 12 months was: _______________.

Now create your intention. Something like this:

I intend to take home ______________ over the next __________ [six months or a year]. I intend to attract this money with ease and grace.

I intend to take my first official paycheck (not a draw) on [date]: ____.

My gross income before expenses for the last four quarters was ____.

With my new goals, intentions, and money mindset in place, I intend to increase those earnings by ______________________ [dollar amount or percentage] over the next four quarters.

APPRECIATE YOUR CURRENT WEALTH

Individuals with a limiting mindset (especially regarding money) tend to focus more on what they *don't* have instead of the abundance they *do* have in their lives. When you learn to emphasize what you already have, rather than what's missing, the resulting attitude of gratitude will raise your energy. Appreciating your current abundance will improve your mood and attitude! As your energy lifts, you'll attract more of the good stuff, including money.

After my devastating financial loss, I felt anger and fear. *Lots* of anger and fear! Every morning, I woke up with anxiety filling my body, and I could only see what was lacking in my life. Fortunately, a gratitude practice turned that around quickly. I call this practice, The Gratitude Shift. In addition to these exercises, I did something really goofy, and I was surprised when it helped.

During this difficult time, I struggled to come up with enough money to pay my hefty property taxes. This was before the fabulous technology that allows us to pay our bills online; I actually wrote checks to pay my charge card minimums and other debts. It wasn't lost on me that every time I had to write a check I was filled with shame, frustration, fear, and even anger, so I kicked my gratitude up a notch in an attempt to break that unhealthy pattern.

While it felt somewhat embarrassing, it was also empowering to write the words, *thank you*, in the memo section of every check. This was my way of acknowledging that I had the money to pay whatever amount I could toward my taxes and other expenses. A simple thank you scrawled on the bottom of a check brought a smile to my face and all but erased the fear in my heart. I'm not sure what the people who opened those payments thought, but I hope it brought a smile to their faces.

Gratitude helped my finances grow stronger. Focusing on the good and doing the gratitude exercise you'll find later in this chapter was the beginning of the end of my misery and financial woes.

FEEL THE WEALTH

I'm sure Dave Ramsey would disagree with me on this, but it's essential to occasionally treat yourself to things that make you feel wealthy. At the same time, it's never wise to repeatedly splurge on things that may be financially out of reach. But a bit of a splurge now and again helps to align us with wealth in a way that makes it feel real and present. The trick is to do it without remorse or guilt!

I had a client—let's call him Craig—who used to drive to his meetings in an old beat-up Chevy. He felt embarrassed and ashamed that despite having helped others become successful, he could only afford a beater. Craig would park his car as far from the meeting as possible to avoid judgment, hoping no one would see him get into or out of it.

My client once believed he would never be able to drive a nice car. The BS story in his head caused embarrassment and emotional pain, and it held him back in more ways than he realized. Naturally, I was determined to help him Bullshift that nonsense, and that's exactly what we did.

Through reframing techniques and by implementing a gratitude practice, Craig learned to appreciate the fact that he at least had reliable transportation. Instead of viewing his excursions with negativity and embarrassment, he said words of gratitude every time he entered his vehicle:

- "I'm grateful to have safe transportation; this car is built like a tank!"

- "I'm thankful I have the means to get to and from my destinations."
- "This old car has been reliable and holds many great memories."

Then we got to work on changing his words and thoughts around his ability to afford a newer, nicer car. Instead of saying, "I will never be able to afford a nice car," he would say, "I'm grateful for the dream car waiting just around the corner" and, "Of course I'll have a new car one day soon."

Again, the magic of the RAS kicked in. As my client shifted his mindset to one of gratitude, releasing his embarrassment and stress, he gained clarity and more motivation. More clients and opportunities came his way. Soon, a friend of a friend decided to sell his gently used luxury car, and my client courageously negotiated terms he could afford with his growing revenues. Just like that, he had a car that he was proud to drive!

This step sparked the confidence and determination that led to tremendous growth for Craig and his company. His small business now shows a monthly gross of about $50,000 with little overhead and high profits. All because he was willing to Bullshift his negative attitude and believe that much more is indeed possible!

Once you show gratitude for what you *do* have rather than resent the absence of what you want, your actions and feelings will reflect your attitude. When you learn to believe in your wealth, whether it's currently present or not, your actions and attitude will reflect your new and improved mindset. When my clients make this shift, wonderful things happen. New clients and customers appear out of nowhere, people pay more, and investors take interest. Because when you believe you're worth more, you *are* seen as being worthy.

Gratitude is a powerful ally in helping our primitive brains transition from the reactive state of survival to the goal of happiness.

Every time you direct your attention toward specific thoughts, you ask your brain to activate those thoughts in the future. This is why gratitude is essential, consistently focusing on positive thoughts creates a positive loop, making happiness possible.

If a pill could simulate the effects of gratitude, everyone would be taking it. Gratitude is one of the most powerful natural mood enhancers available to us, and unlike a pill, it has no negative side effects. Numerous studies have shown its mental and physical benefits. We know that feeling thankful can improve sleep, mood, and immunity, and that gratitude can decrease depression, anxiety, chronic pain, and disease risk.

One recent study found that when expressing gratitude, people avoid pessimism, unhappiness, complaints of malaise and pain, and toxic emotions such as anger, hurt, fear, loneliness, isolation, and lack of engagement. A grateful individual focuses on positive practices of showing solidarity and paying attention to others, and gains a sense of well-being in return.

An excerpt from a Berkeley study on gratitude notes that individuals who participated in the gratitude-writing activities reported better mental health than those who did not participate in any gratitude practice. After just four weeks, the gratitude group showed greater overall well-being. Researchers also found that when participants spent as little as five minutes a day focusing on gratitude for ten weeks, they felt happier, more enthusiastic, and more optimistic about life. In this study of patients with depression and anxiety, those who completed a structured gratitude intervention experienced a measurable decrease in symptoms, compared to those who received no such intervention.

Robert Emmons, Ph.D., an author, researcher, and professor of psychology at the University of California, has dedicated his career to researching gratitude and happiness. According to the scale Emmons used in some studies to calculate well-being, participants who practiced gratitude were a full 25% happier than other participants. Yes, gratitude can make you happier, just like money can make you happier!

Gratitude and happiness go hand in hand, but I am not talking about a robotic recital of a gratitude list. Most of us are already grateful for the obvious things in life: people we love, our health, the roof over our head, food on the table. That kind of gratitude is important, but it does not create transformation. The gratitude practice I am about to introduce goes deeper. It works with the filtering system of your RAS to open your eyes to the small moments, hidden opportunities, and daily evidence that support your growth and success. It trains your mind to look for what is working rather than dwelling on what is not. This practice raises your energy, improves emotional well-being, and rewires your brain for possibility. Through repetition, gratitude activates neuroplasticity and builds new neural pathways that support confidence, resilience, and emotional alignment.

This is not regular gratitude. This is intentional gratitude.

THIS IS THE GRATITUDE SHIFT.

You can make your own Gratitude Shift and engage your subconscious mind with this simple practice.

Step One.

Each day, actively look for three simple things that bring joy to your heart or a smile to your face. This step requires intention and practice, but remember, The Gratitude Shift will retrain your brain to focus on the good rather than the stressful stuff, in the process reprogramming your brain.

Whenever you leave the house, watch for the simple things that bring you a moment of pleasure: a beautiful flower, a sweet interaction between a parent and child, a pleasant smell in the air. Smile at people and invite a simple exchange of pleasantries. These are the small pleasures you're looking for, nothing big and life-changing (yet).

If you stay home for the day, look at your backyard or the sky. Pay attention to a particularly rewarding experience with a client or family member. Heck, this morning, I walked into my bathroom, which I had remodeled last year, and thought about how proud my husband Wally would have been of my tile choices and the other decisions I'd made. I immediately felt gratitude for what my creative and handy husband had taught me about renovations. It's okay to keep it simple! That's the point of The Gratitude Shift.

Notice what you've achieved at work rather than berating yourself for not knocking 10 things off your list. If you have a great meeting or add a prospect to your list, file those achievements away for your gratitude exercise.

Step Two.

Spend five minutes every night recording your three experiences of gratitude in a journal (or journal throughout the day). Again, this isn't just about what you're grateful for; rather, it's about seeking simple reasons to experience gratitude and happiness. You are retraining your brain! These messages of gratitude will overwrite much of your negative thinking.

You don't have to write a novel, a basic sentence or two is perfect. As you record these special moments, allow your heart to feel them all over again. I especially like journaling just before going to sleep. Going to bed happy and filled with gratitude provides many benefits, including a more peaceful night's sleep. This is all a part of The Gratitude Shift.

This exercise is a highly effective way to practice being present in the moment and to teach your brain to seek happiness, not misery.

Here's an example of today's Gratitude Shift for me. I chose to do my writing earlier in the day because I did not want to lose the magic of the energy I felt in that moment.

As I write this passage, it's 10:35 a.m.:

Gratitude Note #1: I bumped into an acquaintance at the coffee shop early this morning. Peter and I hadn't seen one another for a few months, and we had a nice chat to catch up. I am grateful for our friendship and the laughter we shared. It makes my heart feel good.

Gratitude Note #2: This morning, a stranger held the door open for me even though they had to wait a few seconds for me to cross the parking lot. I'm grateful for the kindness that others show to strangers and that I see it everywhere I go.

Gratitude Note #3: I let the dog out at 5 a.m., and it was still dark. I stepped out into the yard, where the moon lit the shadows and shapes surrounding my beautiful pond. I am grateful for the creative inspiration I received to build this place of tranquility and peace with my own hands! I still can't believe I did it. This space is magnificent, especially in the moonlight!

See how easy it is? All of that, and it wasn't even noon yet! I had yet to take a walk to appreciate the beautiful things I would undoubtedly encounter. Or to speak to my clients, who are a constant source of gratitude. By 10:30 a.m., I'd already had so many more opportunities in this day alone to experience the mental and physical benefits of gratitude.

Now it's your turn! Create and recite an intention to be diligent about your gratitude practice for the next seven days. Open your eyes and heart to the beauty you'll find in others, in your relationships, in nature, within yourself, and in your everyday surroundings. Instead of focusing on what you don't have, focus on what you *do* have!

BULLSHIFT EXERCISE 13

Day 1: Today I am grateful for . . .

1. ____

2. ____

3. ____

Day 2: Today I am grateful for . . .

1. ____

2. ____

3. ____

Day 3: Today, I am grateful for . . .

1. ____
____
____

2. ____
____
____

3. ____
____
____

Day 4: Today I am grateful for . . .

1. ____
____
____

2. ____
____
____

3. ____
____
____

Day 5: Today I am grateful for . . .

1. ____

2. ____

3. ____

Day 6: Today I am grateful for . . .

1. ____

2. ____

3. ____

Day 7: Today I am grateful for . . .

1. ______________________________

____

____

2. ______________________________

____

____

3. ______________________________

____

____

WHAT A YEAR OF DOING THE GRATITUDE SHIFT CAN BRING

At first, I relied on the daily journaling exercise to help me focus on the good in my life. After about a year, something remarkable happened. I realized I no longer needed the journal to feel the emotional and mental benefits of gratitude. My mind had learned to notice moments of joy and to experience gratitude naturally. It had become second nature.

Nowadays, I still write down my thoughts of gratitude from time to time, but more often, I simply *live* in a state of awareness and gratitude. I catch the small, beautiful moments as they happen—a smile, a sunset, a tiny win, excitement over an upcoming event. I feel the warmth of these experiences in real time.

That's the power of The Gratitude Shift. It's not just a practice; it becomes a way of being. I invite you to explore it for yourself and see what shifts for you.

SEVEN DAYS OF GRATITUDE LATER

Now that you've opened your eyes and heart to seven days of gratitude, what have you noticed? Have you experienced increased feelings of joy? Less judgment? Any stress reduction, even if it's temporary?

Take a few minutes to write about your Gratitude Shift. Remember, it's only been a week. Continue your practice for a few months to experience how life-changing your gratitude practice can be. I've provided some writing prompts for your next Bullshift exercise should you choose to use them.

BULLSHIFT EXERCISE 14

My Gratitude Shift Observations:

It's been ___________ days/weeks/months since I began The Gratitude Shift.

I've noticed the following benefits.

Check all that apply. These are just food for thought—add your own descriptors, too!

I feel . . .

- ☐ Happier
- ☐ Kinder
- ☐ More present
- ☐ More aware of joy in my body
- ☐ More patient
- ☐ More aware of how much there is to be grateful for
- ☐ Lighter
- ☐ More curious
- ☐ More inspired

- ☐ More focused and clear
- ☐ Calmer throughout the day or at bedtime
- ☐ Less irritable/agitated
- ☐ Less depressed/sad
- ☐ Less anxious
- ☐ Less forgetful
- ☐ Less stressed

What else have you noticed since beginning The Gratitude Shift work? Write your observations here:

____

____

____

____

____

I intend to continue my gratitude work for at least ____________.

At the beginning of your Gratitude Shift, you may want to set a daily reminder until you become accustomed to your new intention of living in gratitude.

I will set my reminders for (what time of the day). ______________.

THE ADDED BENEFITS OF THE GRATITUDE SHIFT

Be sure to practice self-awareness as you increase your vibration of gratitude. A daily gratitude practice can profoundly transform your mindset and overall well-being! Here are some added benefits to look for:

1. **Improved mental health:** Gratitude helps shift your focus away from negative thoughts and feelings. Regularly reflecting on

what you're grateful for reduces anxiety, stress, and depression, leading to a more positive and resilient mental state.

2. **Increased happiness:** Focusing on the good in your life, no matter how small, boosts overall feelings of happiness and contentment. Studies show that people who practice gratitude consistently report higher levels of life satisfaction.
3. **Stronger relationships:** Expressing gratitude strengthens your connections with others. When you acknowledge and appreciate people in your life, you foster deeper bonds with them, leading to stronger personal and professional relationships.
4. **Better sleep:** A gratitude practice (especially at night!) can help calm your mind and reduce stress, leading to improved sleep quality. Reflecting on positive things before bed shifts your focus away from worries, making it easier to relax.
5. **Boosted self-esteem:** Gratitude encourages you to appreciate your own achievements and qualities, fostering greater self-worth and confidence. You begin to recognize your value and accomplishments more clearly, leading to a healthier self-image.
6. **Increased resilience:** Gratitude helps you maintain a positive outlook even during challenging times. By focusing on what you still have rather than on what's lacking, you build resilience to navigate adversity with grace.
7. **Enhanced physical health:** Gratitude is linked to healthier behaviors like exercising regularly, eating better, and tending to medical advice. It also helps lower blood pressure and boosts your immune system by reducing your stress levels.

Incorporating a gratitude practice into your daily routine can create a ripple effect, improving your internal state and your interactions with the world around you. Your money tree will thrive in this environment!

Gratitude changes everything. It shifts your energy. It rewires your brain. It trains your RAS to look for opportunity instead of limitation. When you commit to The Gratitude Shift, you become a magnet for abundance. So, keep going. Stay intentional. Let gratitude set the tone for your success. Now that you have anchored abundance inside you, it is time to bring that same energy to your business and water your money tree like you mean it.

CHAPTER 16
Water Your Money Tree

For generations, many of us have been taught that *saving money for a rainy day* is essential. While being prepared for the unexpected seems like sound advice, the idea often stems from a place of fear and scarcity—it represents an underlying belief that financial struggles are inevitable and that we should brace ourselves for them. But this scarcity mindset limits us, keeping us stuck in a cycle of worry and lack. Instead, let's shift to a mindset of abundance, where we trust in the flow of money and our ability to attract it effortlessly. Believe that your savings and investments will add up in no time and build from there. Know without a doubt that you will have money to invest in your business, to play with, and to provide for your family. With this mindset in place, your money tree will be well-tended.

> **Repeat to yourself:**
> ***"I have money. More money will come! Money flows easily into my life and I will always have more than enough."***

Affirmations like this are not wishful thinking. They are instructions for your brain. When you speak these words with intention, you begin training your subconscious to expect abundance rather than fear and lack. Your energy shifts, your decisions improve, and you are more confident, which opens your mind to income-generating opportunities.

Do what you can to save money, even if your money mindset is not yet fully abundant. When you save, do it with optimism and excitement instead of fear. Saving from a place of anxiety feeds scarcity. Saving from a place of power builds wealth.

IT'S OKAY TO START SMALL

I used to think that saving a few cents a day would not make a difference, but it adds up. Once you achieve a small savings goal, you build momentum and reach higher targets. You begin to trust yourself with money. You see that saving is not difficult and that you are capable of building wealth one step at a time. Every deposit, no matter how small, strengthens your belief in abundance and grows another healthy root in your money tree.

I started my new savings in one of those little jars that register the "deposit" with a readout of the balance in the jar. Watching it add up was entertaining and created a sense of control over my finances. I began this practice years ago, after The Fat Bean fiasco, when I didn't have money to spare, and I still do it now just for fun! I love watching the coins add up to dollars, and when the jar hits its limit, I cash it in for something I consider to be a memorable experience or splurge. It's a celebratory event. I just bought myself a lovely silver bracelet from Italy, what a treat!

Rather than approaching your savings with a rigid mindset, make it a little competitive and enjoyable. How can you turn saving money into a game? Find a friend eager to grow their financial abundance and turn it into a friendly competition. Or involve your family and create a savings challenge where everyone works toward milestones, jointly celebrating with small rewards or activities as each person reaches their goals.

I have a friend with three young children, and she's brilliant at turning everyday responsibilities like saving money, doing chores, and even brushing teeth into fun, competitive activities. For example, the child who completes all their chores by the end of the week gets to pick the game for family game night or decide what's for dinner. The kids love these challenges, which motivates them to stay on top of their responsibilities.

When the family was planning a vacation to Disney World, my friend turned saving money into a family project. She labeled a manila envelope "Vacation Fund" and made it clear that any extra spending money for the trip would come from what they saved in the envelope over the next eight months. Whenever one of the kids wanted fast food or to go on a costly outing, she gave them a choice: spend the money now or put it toward their Disney fund. She'd ask, "Would you rather have McDonald's tonight or save that money so we can have lunch with Mickey Mouse?"

The strategy worked! The kids happily chose homemade meals, and Mom let them tuck the would-be McDonald's money into the Disney envelope. It turned saving into a fun, collaborative effort. Before long, the kids were donating their allowances to the vacation fund, predicting what exciting things they would do on their family vacation.

Be creative with your savings goals, whether you're saving hundreds of dollars or thousands of dollars. As your nest egg grows, be sure you put your money into something that generates interest. (Don't put it into a checking account!) It's best to keep your money tree savings at a different financial institution than the bank where you regularly do business. I keep mine in an online account that allows me to create sub-accounts for various savings purposes. I create accounts for home repairs and projects, vacations, new cars as needed, and fun outings. These are all exciting goals, making it easier to put money into an account as I envision my goals coming to fruition. Last year, I went to Italy for a month, and there was no financial sting because the money was already there. It's far more fun to vacation without money worries dictating your choices. I had the time of my life on my dream vacation!

IDENTIFY YOUR SAVINGS GOAL, ALONG WITH THE INTENTION TO ACHIEVE IT WITH EASE

Like anything, if you believe that saving money is difficult, well, then it is. If you think the little money you can put away won't matter in the long run, it won't. Your thoughts dictate your reality, so why not think positively and see what happens?

In a previous chapter, I spoke of my client Craig who purchased a much-needed upgraded car. Once he decided which car he wanted, he envisioned the joy of driving it, keeping it shiny and clean, and parking wherever he wished rather than a block away from his destination. He decided he would soon drive a nice car; from there, the rest felt accessible. Craig diligently watered his money tree by maintaining his positive attitude and stashing away small amounts of cash for his car purchase. He was on a roll! New money-making ideas kept flowing, and he created a pricing model for his services that properly reflected his value. Soon it was even easier to make more money, thereby making it easier to save more money!

In short, create a goal, name it, believe in it, visualize it, feel grateful for its existence, and make it fun. Then, watch your money tree grow!

BULLSHIFT EXERCISE 15

Use this page to name your intentions and savings goals.

I intend to save $ ______________ in [how many weeks, months] ____.

I intend to save or invest my money [where] _________________ ____.

I intend to [do what with] _______________________ some of my savings.

I intend to attract and save money with ease!

Once you identify your goal, stop what you are doing, go online, and open an interest-bearing account. Create a mini vision board with images of your soon-to-be purchases and financial achievements. Express daily gratitude for your abundance and enjoy knowing that your goal is as good as done. You now know how to grow personal wealth through clarity, discipline, and intention. In the next chapter, we will take this same mindset and apply it to your business so your money tree can expand in every direction.

CHAPTER 17

How to Leverage Bullshift into Business Success

You have started growing your personal wealth, but now it is time to strengthen the financial health of your business. I am willing to bet there are areas of your business where you are losing money, leaving profit on the table, or missing opportunities for financial growth. When entrepreneurs struggle financially, they become overwhelmed and that stress affects decision-making, productivity, and energy. The good news is that you can change this.

When you find yourself in an emotional and stressful moment, do your best to pause and apply what you've learned: do breathwork, reframe your thoughts, find your truth instead of adding to your negativity, visualize something exciting or peaceful, repeat positive affirmations, and remind yourself that *you have the power to change your thoughts, and therefore, your reality.*

MINDSET IN MOTION

Think about the things you avoid in your business because paying attention to them causes you stress. You may tell yourself you're too busy or you don't want the stress of learning something new, like understanding your financial statements or implementing the use of a CRM (client relationship management tool). You might avoid prospecting or networking because it feels uncomfortable. Such avoidance will hold you back from the success you deserve! Let's take a look at the pain caused by your avoidance, should you have any.

BULLSHIFT EXERCISE 16, PART ONE

Can you list ten things you have been procrastinating on and why (be honest with yourself!)?

1. I have been procrastinating on ______________________

   ____

   because ____

   ____.

2. I have been procrastinating on ______________________

   ____

   because ____

   ____.

3. I have been procrastinating on ______________________

   ____

   because ____

   ____.

4. I have been procrastinating on ______________________

   ____

   because ____

   ____.

5. I have been procrastinating on ____________________
____
because _______________________________________
____.

6. I have been procrastinating on ____________________
____
because _______________________________________
____.

7. I have been procrastinating on ____________________
____
because _______________________________________
____.

8. I have been procrastinating on ____________________
____
because _______________________________________
____.

9. I have been procrastinating on ____________________
____
because _______________________________________
____.

10. I have been procrastinating on ____________________
____
because _______________________________________
____.

Good! Now look at your list to identify which items you've been avoiding due to a limiting belief. For example, I knew I had to network more but I would tell myself that local networking was stupid because my ideal clients didn't exist in my hometown. My hometown has a population of about 155,000. I'm not sure how I convinced myself of that lie!

The tendency to make excuses for the things we don't want to do comes from our protective instincts. If I believed that no ideal clients lived in or near my hometown, I wouldn't have to face the discomfort of walking into a networking event filled with strangers. I could avoid the small talk that I disdain. I could avoid the possibility that I wasn't bright or charming enough to attract someone interesting who may have needed my help. Yes, my limiting thoughts stemmed from my brain trying to protect me from failure.

Let's look at the cost of *your* avoidance and procrastination. What activities on your procrastination list are essential to your business growth, your relationships, and/or your well-being? Honestly? It's probably everything you listed! For each of them, write a sentence or two that addresses the consequences of your avoidance. For example, if you've been meaning to develop a marketing strategy, what's the cost to you and your business when you put it off? If you now know that you must restructure your pricing model (because you're worth so much more) but haven't, what is the cost to your business and your sense of self-worth? If you don't make time for exercise, going to the doctor, and pursuing general self-care routines, what might the consequences be? Let's find out.

BULLSHIFT EXERCISE 16, PART TWO

Go through the items on your procrastination list and explore how delaying them affects you and your business. Is there a cost beyond you and your business? Your procrastination may be affecting your family or other important people in your life.

This exercise is not intended to bring you emotional pain, but to help you realize how much power you hold to create positive change!

1. The potential pain and cost of procrastinating on ____________ ______________________ is ____________________________________ ____.

2. The potential pain and cost of procrastinating on ____________ ______________________ is ____________________________________ ____.

3. The potential pain and cost of procrastinating on ____________ ______________________ is ____________________________________ ____.

4. The potential pain and cost of procrastinating on ____________ ______________________ is ____________________________________ ____.

5. The potential pain and cost of procrastinating on ____________ ______________________ is ____________________________________ ____.

6. The potential pain and cost of procrastinating on ____________ ______________________ is ____________________________________ ____.

7. The potential pain and cost of procrastinating on ____________ ______________________ is ____________________________________ ____.

8. The potential pain and cost of procrastinating on ______________________________ is ____.

9. The potential pain and cost of procrastinating on ______________________________ is ____.

10. The potential pain and cost of procrastinating on ______________________________ is ____.

Hopefully seeing the impact of your procrastination in writing will help you strategize a plan to prioritize and act on your list! You may need support, though. The belief that we can or must do this alone is another common misconception among entrepreneurs. This is when you need to find a great business coach, mentor, and/or other means of support. Your progress will march along quickly and efficiently with proper support resources in your life and business.

KNOW YOUR NUMBERS

I see a lot of financial avoidance among entrepreneurs. Do you review your Profit and Loss statement, receivables, and cash flow every month? Do you know your numbers—*really* know what they mean and how to use the data to make informed decisions? Do you know where you spend your money and whether your efforts are cost-effective? Do you have a clear understanding of your expenses and pricing model?

Many of my new clients don't fully understand their numbers. It's not a comprehension issue because entrepreneurs are smart people! It's the issue of avoidance and fear that causes the problem. After all, what you don't know can't hurt you, right? Wrong. Knowledge is power. Avoiding tough truths, like poor profit margins and the inefficiencies that cause them, only delays taking necessary actions. The longer you wait, the worse it gets.

Today I spoke with a client who took my advice and met with his accountant to discuss his business finances. He knew the business hadn't done well at the beginning of the year, but he'd been unaware that he was operating at a deficit, meaning his expenses were higher than his income. During the eight months we've been working together thus far, he repaired most of the flaws in his system and is no longer losing money, but there's one thing he hadn't done: take action to generate new business. His limiting beliefs were keeping him from calling past clients, potential strategic partners, and other influencers in his industry to create more leads and prospects. So, while the holes in his business were patched, he wasn't fertilizing his money tree by doing the right activities to add more revenue. It couldn't flourish, let alone survive much longer.

We chipped away at his belief that calling people would not make a difference, and his conversation with his accountant gave him the wake-up call he needed. Guess what? He spent the next two days on the phone successfully drumming up business. Now he'll make up his shortfall and end the year in the black rather than deeper into the red. And now that he has experienced success in this business-building technique, he'll do more of it.

The truth may be brutal to face at times, but you cannot change your reality until you embrace it. Know your numbers, make the difficult decisions, and do more of what works.

ACCOUNTS RECEIVABLE

Do not overlook your accounts receivable. It is a key part of your financial health. Struggling entrepreneurs who offer a service are known to continue working on jobs and for clients even when the customer has past-due invoices. This behavior is based on a scarcity mindset. These entrepreneurs are thinking one or more of the following:

- *What if the client leaves?*
- *I don't like confrontation—I won't say anything, and I'll just hope they pay up!*
- *I'll go broke if I lose this client!*

But here's the hard truth: a client who is 90 days or more overdue on their invoices is unlikely to pay you—ever. Your scarcity mindset, not the deadbeat clients, is what will bring down your business. Studies show that the longer an invoice remains unpaid, the less likely it is to be collected.

While there's no guarantee, proactive steps like frequent communication, offering payment plans, or even involving a collection agency will help improve the chances of collecting on overdue accounts. However, the most effective solution is to prevent invoices from becoming overdue in the first place. Also, discontinue services if even just one invoice is overdue. Some entrepreneurs fall into the trap of providing services in hopes of the client eventually catching up on overdue charges . Again, this is your scarcity mindset coming to the surface. Always withhold services when fees are due.

This topic takes us back to the question of value and self-worth. Why is your client more deserving than you are? If you don't respect and claim your value, no one else will.

HOLDING ON FOR THE SAKE OF HOLDING ON

As you cultivate a growth mindset, take a fresh look at your resources—contractors, employees, vendors, and professional service providers like your accountant and bookkeeper. Many entrepreneurs hold on to resources that no longer serve their needs, often out of guilt or because they feel too overwhelmed to deal with the hassle of making changes. But as your business grows, it's natural, and necessary, to outgrow certain people and services along the way.

- Your right-hand person—the Jack or Jill of all trades—may grow resentful as you bring in other human resources. A more advanced business model may be over their heads, or perhaps they liked the business just as it was and won't do well with change.
- The company you once purchased supplies from can't offer volume discounts as your demand grows, and they cannot match their competitor's pricing.
- Your once-trustworthy accountant (who may have been doing your family taxes for a decade or more) isn't well-versed in business accounting.

Letting go, whether it's letting go of outdated thought patterns or people who no longer align with your growth strategy, will feel more natural as you embrace your new mindset and leadership role. Difficult decisions are part of every entrepreneur's journey, but as your mindset and prosperity grow, so will your confidence in making those tough choices.

HIRE THE RIGHT HELP

What would you do with the time if you could add 20 hours to your weekly clock to focus only on growth strategies, thus increasing your business revenues? Do you have a list of activities that would most likely lead to growth?

Most entrepreneurs answer yes to that last question: They know how to grow their business but aren't doing it. That happens for many reasons, including an unhealthy money mindset and other limiting beliefs held by struggling entrepreneurs. For the sake of this exercise, we're going to look at one of the most crippling and common negative mindset themes lurking in the heads of small business owners: a refusal to hire contractors or employees.

We make up all sorts of reasons to avoid asking for help. Here are the most common reasons, actually excuses:

- I can't afford to hire help.
- No one else will do it right, so I need to do everything myself.
- Employees are a pain in the a$$!
- You can't find good help anymore.
- I don't want the responsibility of having employees.
- I don't have enough work to keep them busy.
- I don't have time to teach someone how to do these things—it's easier and faster to do it myself.

Do any of these beliefs have a familiar ring? In Chapter 1, I said, "Here's the thing: when people have a negative belief system, they don't often realize it because it's their reality."

Your perspective may be based on what you learned under challenging circumstances in the past, or what you were taught by your parents and other influential people in your life. Perhaps you had a negative experience when you outsourced to a freelancer. Maybe you tried to find the perfect addition to your team and all the applicants let you down. Or, as in the case of one of my group coaching clients, Vivian, you've witnessed a peer or relative struggle with managing a team or even a single employee.

Vivian came from a family of successful architects, but she chose to become a family law attorney. She was exhausted because she was working around the clock and was not reaping the financial rewards for her efforts. But for Vivian, hiring an employee was entirely out of the question. "I've seen my brother and sister-in-law struggle with their employees for 10 years," she told me. "They have a team of 15 and wish they could return to doing everything themselves. They say life was easier then."

When I asked Vivian about the culture her brother and sister-in-law had developed for their architectural firm, I was met with a blank stare. "You know what I mean," I said, "the values, beliefs, behaviors, and practices that shape how their employees interact with each other and their clients—your brother and sister-in-law's leadership and communication styles and how they establish expectations for their employees and for themselves as employers."

Vivian firmly shook her head and said her family's firm had never considered any of those things. Of course they hadn't. I knew that before I asked her the culture question, because their frustration and struggles were a dead giveaway. Entrepreneurs who do not build a positive, intentional culture struggle with success. Instead of a happy team working like a well-oiled machine, these entrepreneurs are likely to have constant miscommunication, low morale, poor accountability, and a revolving door of employees who feel undervalued and uninspired.

My client's entire belief system about hiring employees had been shaped by her brother and sister-in-law's leadership failures because that was the only reality she knew. I hope that going forward, Vivian will form her own opinions and shape her future experiences based on what she learns during coaching sessions rather than let her relatives' failing business model influence her decisions.

I CAN'T AFFORD TO HIRE HELP

If you're self-employed and managing every part of your business independently but you want to grow, it's worth considering why you haven't yet hired at least one employee or brought in a few freelancers to help. Usually, business owners hide behind the belief that they cannot afford to pay anyone to do the work they can do themselves. My argument is that you cannot **not** afford to hire someone. I'll walk you through the process (including doing the math) to assist you in changing your BS mindset about asking for, and paying for, help.

This next Bullshift exercise will take place over five days. Use the tracking sheets provided to write down how you spend your time at work. There are also tracking software applications out there if you prefer to automate this task. Either way, track *everything!* Log how much time you spend on each task and whether you resolve it. Also, categorize each task into one of the categories listed at the top of each page using the number related to each category. Bear with me! This is tedious, yes, but this critical exercise will teach you a lot.

BULLSHIFT EXERCISE 17, PART ONE

Monday

Zone		Activity	Start time	End time	Result
1	Administrative tasks				
2	Client fulfillment services				
3	Email and text message management				
4	Errands and miscellaneous				
5	Data entry/ managing inventory/order processing				
6	Misc. phone calls and voicemails				
7	Website maintenance				

Zone		Activity	Start time	End time	Result
8	Event planning				
9	Invoicing, proposals, expenses, and bookkeeping services				
10	Customer support/client communication				
11	Research				
12	Product and supply sourcing/ordering				
13	Technical issues and basic enhancements				
14	Sales activities/client acquisitions				
15	Product and service development				

Zone		Activity	Start time	End time	Result
16	Strategic planning activities/vision/ long-term goals				
17	Networking opportunities				
18	Leadership and personal development				
19	Assessing market conditions to identify necessary changes				
20	Public speaking/ personal branding/thought management				
21	Client retention strategies				
22	Team building and leadership				
23	Financial strategy and investment				

Zone		Activity	Start time	End time	Result
24	High-level marketing strategies and brand building				
25	Other [specify]				
26					
27					
28					
29					

Tuesday

Zone		Activity	Start time	End time	Result
1	Administrative tasks				
2	Client fulfillment services				
3	Email and text message management				
4	Errands and miscellaneous				
5	Data entry/ managing inventory/order processing				
6	Misc. phone calls and voicemails				
7	Website maintenance				

Zone		Activity	Start time	End time	Result
8	Event planning				
9	Invoicing, proposals, expenses, and bookkeeping services				
10	Customer support/client communication				
11	Research				
12	Product and supply sourcing/ordering				
13	Technical issues and basic enhancements				
14	Sales activities/client acquisitions				
15	Product and service development				

Zone		Activity	Start time	End time	Result
16	Strategic planning activities/vision/ long-term goals				
17	Networking opportunities				
18	Leadership and personal development				
19	Assessing market conditions to identify necessary changes				
20	Public speaking/ personal branding/thought management				
21	Client retention strategies				
22	Team building and leadership				
23	Financial strategy and investment				

Zone		Activity	Start time	End time	Result
24	High-level marketing strategies and brand building				
25	Other [specify]				
26					
27					
28					
29					

Wednesday

Zone		Activity	Start time	End time	Result
1	Administrative tasks				
2	Client fulfillment services				
3	Email and text message management				
4	Errands and miscellaneous				
5	Data entry/ managing inventory/order processing				
6	Misc. phone calls and voicemails				
7	Website maintenance				

Zone		Activity	Start time	End time	Result
8	Event planning				
9	Invoicing, proposals, expenses, and bookkeeping services				
10	Customer support/client communication				
11	Research				
12	Product and supply sourcing/ordering				
13	Technical issues and basic enhancements				
14	Sales activities/client acquisitions				
15	Product and service development				

Zone		Activity	Start time	End time	Result
16	Strategic planning activities/vision/ long-term goals				
17	Networking opportunities				
18	Leadership and personal development				
19	Assessing market conditions to identify necessary changes				
20	Public speaking/ personal branding/thought management				
21	Client retention strategies				
22	Team building and leadership				
23	Financial strategy and investment				

Zone		Activity	Start time	End time	Result
24	High-level marketing strategies and brand building				
25	Other [specify]				
26					
27					
28					
29					

Thursday

Zone		Activity	Start time	End time	Result
1	Administrative tasks				
2	Client fulfillment services				
3	Email and text message management				
4	Errands and miscellaneous				
5	Data entry/ managing inventory/order processing				
6	Misc. phone calls and voicemails				
7	Website maintenance				

Zone		Activity	Start time	End time	Result
8	Event planning				
9	Invoicing, proposals, expenses, and bookkeeping services				
10	Customer support/client communication				
11	Research				
12	Product and supply sourcing/ordering				
13	Technical issues and basic enhancements				
14	Sales activities/client acquisitions				
15	Product and service development				

Zone		Activity	Start time	End time	Result
16	Strategic planning activities/vision/ long-term goals				
17	Networking opportunities				
18	Leadership and personal development				
19	Assessing market conditions to identify necessary changes				
20	Public speaking/ personal branding/thought management				
21	Client retention strategies				
22	Team building and leadership				
23	Financial strategy and investment				

Zone		Activity	Start time	End time	Result
24	High-level marketing strategies and brand building				
25	Other [specify]				
26					
27					
28					
29					

Friday

Zone		Activity	Start time	End time	Result
1	Administrative tasks				
2	Client fulfillment services				
3	Email and text message management				
4	Errands and miscellaneous				
5	Data entry/ managing inventory/order processing				
6	Misc. phone calls and voicemails				
7	Website maintenance				

Zone		Activity	Start time	End time	Result
8	Event planning				
9	Invoicing, proposals, expenses, and bookkeeping services				
10	Customer support/client communication				
11	Research				
12	Product and supply sourcing/ordering				
13	Technical issues and basic enhancements				
14	Sales activities/client acquisitions				
15	Product and service development				

Zone		Activity	Start time	End time	Result
16	Strategic planning activities/vision/ long-term goals				
17	Networking opportunities				
18	Leadership and personal development				
19	Assessing market conditions to identify necessary changes				
20	Public speaking/ personal branding/thought management				
21	Client retention strategies				
22	Team building and leadership				
23	Financial strategy and investment				

Zone		Activity	Start time	End time	Result
24	High-level marketing strategies and brand building				
25	Other [specify]				
26					
27					
28					
29					

FIVE DAYS LATER

Hopefully you've tracked your time for five days by now. Let's see what we can learn from your data! As an entrepreneur, you have one job: to grow your business. So here are the pivotal questions:

- How many hours have you spent in the past five days on activities that will make a meaningful impact on your business?
- How much of that time was dedicated to actions that will directly increase your revenue?
- Did you grow your prospect list or add new customers to your client base?
- Did you work on an exciting marketing project or develop a plan to launch your next big initiative?

Looking at the list of activities provided, how much time was spent on tasks numbered 1 through 13? This is the **loss zone,** where you're losing money if you perform these jobs yourself. We need to create an environment where you can focus your time in the **profit zone,** numbers 14 through 24. That's where your true value lies!

Calculate how much time on average you spend on the money-making activities in the profit zone. If you're a coach, therapist, accountant, photographer, lawyer, or any other type of service provider, you'll spend time with clients, and that's unavoidable (to a degree). This time counts as a money-making activity, i.e., the profit zone. However, if the remainder of your time is tied up in work that can be outsourced (in the loss zone) you're limiting your income potential.

Let's say you spent 20 hours on the non-entrepreneurial tasks in the loss zone. What if you could devote those 20 hours to growing your client/customer base by staying in your profit zone?

Most entrepreneurs do not realize how much time they lose on tasks that do not move the business forward. That lost time is lost money. When you spread yourself thin doing administrative work, low-value tasks, or work someone else could do for a lower rate, you stunt your revenue and burn yourself out. Those hours could be used for activities that generate income, build your brand, deepen client relationships, and open doors to new opportunities.

In the second half of this Bullshift exercise, let's discover what you could do with the time you are wasting on non-entrepreneurial activities in the loss zone. This exercise is designed to help you overcome the limiting belief that you must do everything on your own. Use this guideline to identify activities that will help you increase revenues and solidify your business model.

BULLSHIFT EXERCISE 17, PART TWO

Looking at your time tracking sheets, how many hours did you spend over the last five days in your loss zone? ________________

What could you do with that time if you had that number of hours to spend **ON** your business, generating new business, instead of **IN** your business?

____

____

____

____

____

Before you move on, take a moment to really look at the number of lost hours you wrote above. Those hours represent *opportunity.* That is time you could reclaim and reinvest into high-value activities that actually grow your business. Most entrepreneurs say they do not have time to work on their business, but the reality is that they are simply spending their time in the wrong places. When you shift even a few of those hours from your loss zone into your profit zone, everything begins to change. You gain momentum. You feel more in control. You begin to see what is truly possible for your business. To help you make that shift, we will use the Small Business Growth Activities list later in this chapter as inspiration, but first, let's explore what is truly possible when you invest your time wisely.

THE POWER OF RECLAIMING YOUR TIME

When I ask my clients how quickly they could grow their revenues with the proper support in place, the most common response is two to three months, so we'll use that timeframe for this next exercise.

Let's just say that hiring a part-time virtual or in-house administrative assistant who would take 20 hours of tasks off your plate per week could cost around $1,500 to $2,000 per month. Your next goal is to save enough money for one or two months of your new contractor's wages. This is where your BS stories might start rearing their ugly heads:

- I don't have a few grand just lying around.
- There isn't any good help out there.
- I don't have that kind of time! It would take me three months to train someone.

Use your Bullshift tools, especially your realistic magic wand. What if you could find someone amazing to work with you? What if you already know someone who could do the job? What if you know someone willing to invest some money in your business? What if you have outstanding receivables you could collect?

By challenging your negative thought patterns, you'll open your mind to possibilities and become a more creative problem-solver. Also, it's time to challenge your part-lie, part-truth statements, like "I don't have that kind of time! Training someone would take me three months." It may be true that you don't *currently* have much time, but that's precisely what we're working to change. Success relies on your willingness to stretch your mind, get out of your comfort zone, and inspire change. Would it *really* take three months to train someone to run errands, manage emails, edit content, and do the bookkeeping? Of course they'll take time to get up to speed, but your new person will relieve parts of your work burden faster than you believe they will right now.

In all my years of coaching, I've seen this strategy fail only a handful of times. In one case, my client hired not one but three team members within two months. That's rapid growth, and she wasn't ready, despite giving things her best shot. Take it slow and create training materials as you go along. Your new assistant can take notes and create a training manual for their position, making your future onboarding efforts more efficient.

I recall another occasion when a client hadn't developed a growth plan before hiring his assistant. Instead, he chose to take time away from the office because it felt so good to have more free time. I understood his need for a break, but his plan failed. Don't let that be you! Be diligent and determined. Get your mindset on and make this happen!

YOUR PROFIT ZONE STARTS HERE

These are examples of revenue-generating, strategic, and business-building actions that create real progress. Review the list and select the activities that will have the greatest impact on your growth, then personalize it for your business and industry.

Small Business Growth Activities

1. Strategic planning and vision setting
    - Business vision and long-term goals: Spend time setting and refining your company's long-term vision and goals.
    - Strategic planning: Regularly evaluate the direction of your business and adjust strategies as necessary.

- Market trends and competitor analysis: To make wise decisions, stay informed about industry trends and competitors.

2. Business development
   - Client acquisition: Focus on networking, meeting with prospects, and closing deals.
   - Expand relationships: Build and nurture relationships with key partners, stakeholders, and high-value clients.
   - Identify new opportunities: Actively seek new revenue streams, partnerships, and/or areas for expansion.

3. Product or service innovation
   - Improve offerings: Dedicate time to improving your products or services, ensuring that they meet market needs and exceed customer expectations.
   - Research and development: Explore innovative solutions, new technologies, and/or services that could give your business a competitive edge.

4. Marketing and branding
   - High-level marketing strategy: Focus on crafting and refining your overall marketing strategy, ensuring alignment with your brand and goals.
   - Content creation and campaign direction: Oversee the development of key marketing campaigns that strengthen brand visibility and drive sales.
   - Brand building: Ensure that your brand communicates its value effectively and stays relevant to your target audience.

5. Financial oversight and growth
    - Financial strategy: Spend time understanding the numbers—cash flow, profit margins, and cost management—and planning for financial growth.
    - Investment decisions: Evaluate opportunities to reinvest profits, explore funding options, and/or expand the business.
    - Revenue-generating activities: Focus on activities and decisions that directly lead to sales growth and increased profitability.

6. Team building and leadership
    - Hire key talent: Take an active role in hiring top talent that aligns with your vision and can help scale your business.
    - Leadership development: Invest in developing your leadership skills and those of your key team members.
    - Build company culture: Foster a positive company culture that motivates and retains talent, driving both productivity and loyalty.

7. Delegation and empowerment
    - Delegate effectively: Focus on high-level tasks and delegate administrative, operational, and/or non-revenue-generating activities to others.
    - Empower your team: Ensure that your team has the tools, resources, and autonomy to succeed, allowing you to focus on growth.

8. Customer relations and retention
    - Customer feedback: Actively seek customer feedback to ensure that you meet their needs and exceed their expectations.
    - Client retention strategies: Develop programs or strategies to retain loyal customers and increase lifetime customer value.

9. Networking and relationship building
    - Industry networking: Build strong relationships with industry peers, influencers, and mentors to stay connected to opportunities.
    - Public speaking and thought leadership: Position yourself as a thought leader by speaking at events, writing, and/or participating in podcasts or webinars.

10. Personal development and well-being
    - Continuous learning: Invest in personal development through reading, attending workshops, and/or working with coaches to enhance your skills.
    - Mindset and mental health: Prioritize self-care and a growth mindset to avoid burnout and maintain the energy you need for your entrepreneurial journey.

11. Risk management and adaptability
    - Crisis management and problem-solving: Focus on proactively identifying and solving potential business problems before they escalate.
    - Adapt to change: Spend time learning how to stay flexible and adapt your business model when market conditions change.

Mini Bullshift Journaling Prompt:

List your customized growth activities here:

____

____

____

____

____

____

____

____

____

____

____

____

____

If you had the time to implement your growth strategy, how quickly could you increase your revenues by, let's say, 10% to 15%?

____.

How you use your time determines your results, but how you show up determines your long-term success.

Nurture your money tree with honesty and integrity in your business. Be willing to confront the tough challenges that come your way because no matter the situation, you *can* adapt and improve. Avoiding problems only breeds fear, and fear invites anxiety and stress, and anxiety and fear can cloud your judgment and prevent you from operating at your best.

Your business will only grow as strong as your mindset allows. Strategy matters, but mindset fuels consistent action. Let's return to the Bullshift Process so you can stay grounded, focused, and in control of your energy as you scale your business.

CHAPTER 18

Bullshift for Life

Let's revisit the Bullshift Process, a growth-minded approach that's simple but not always easy. Simplicity can be deceptive, and people often let these practices fall by the wayside, especially when the results, though profound, can be subtle at first. Change happens gradually, but when it hits, you'll know! By consistently practicing the Bullshift exercises in this book, you'll notice a shift—a return to your authentic self, unburdened by stress and worries.

The work on your growth mindset is not a one-and-done deal. Worry and anxiety will creep back in if you stop nurturing yourself, like weeds overtaking an untended garden. Keep tending to your growth and the growth of your money tree.

OWN YOUR POWER AND TAKE ACTION

By now you have already proven that you can shift your thoughts, calm your nervous system, rewrite your beliefs, and take powerful action. You now understand how to nurture your money tree with intention, purpose, and courage. You are no longer circling the loop of scarcity; you are creating your own path to abundance. Now the question is no longer "Will my business grow?" The new question is, "How far am I willing to go?"

The next level of success requires a new level of thinking, and sometimes the fastest way to rise is to get guidance from someone who has been there.

Seeking guidance from an expert is not a sign of weakness; it's an investment in yourself. A good coach or mentor will give you the insight, emotional support, and tools you need, and the return on your investment will be well worth it. Over time, many of my clients have grown from the low six figures well into the seven-figure revenue zone. You can, too! Consider the reduced stress, the peace of mind, increased personal time, and overall happiness. You just can't put a price tag on any of this!

CONSIDER ADDITIONAL TOOLS AND APPROACHES

When you are ready for an even more profound transformation, explore techniques like Emotional Freedom Techniques (EFT), Eye Movement Desensitization and Reprocessing (EMDR), hypnosis, or Cognitive Behavioral Therapy (CBT). These tools unlock emotional roadblocks that hold you back from success. Professionally and personally, EFT tapping has been my secret weapon. This powerful technique involves gently tapping on specific acupressure points while focusing on negative emotions. It helps release emotional charge from old memories and limiting beliefs, allowing you to rewire your brain and create space for healthier thoughts and behaviors.

EFT has had a profound impact on my coaching clients and their businesses. I have watched entrepreneurs dissolve lifelong fears of visibility, money, leadership, and rejection—sometimes in a single session. I have seen clients double their monthly revenue after clearing emotional blocks that were sabotaging their decisions. Others finally raised their prices, hired support, or launched long-postponed offers once the emotional weight of self-doubt was lifted. EFT does more than calm your nervous system. It frees your mind so you can take bold, aligned action without emotional resistance. That is what creates fast, lasting transformation.

Find what works for you and use it to fuel your growth.

MAKE THE DECISION TO CHANGE

The most important step toward mindset mastery is your decision to create real and lasting change. Understand that you don't have to stay stuck where you are. Instead, you can empower yourself with action. The moment you make the decision to grow, your mind will open to new possibilities and solutions will start to appear. No matter your current circumstances, you have choices. Ask yourself: What choice feels most empowering right now?

You now have everything you need to transform your mindset, your money, and your life—but this work only works if you do it. Do not just read this book. Live it. Use the Bullshift exercises daily. Keep challenging your thoughts. Keep setting intentions. Keep nurturing your money tree. Momentum begins with consistent action.

If you are ready for deeper transformation and want support as you rise to your next level of success, I would be honored to be your guide. You do not have to do this alone. Connect with me at *www.marlatabaka.com* and let's continue this journey together.

OWN YOUR WORTH

I want you to walk away from this book knowing your true value. You bring something extraordinary to the world, don't forget that! When you align yourself with what you want and deserve, life shifts in your favor. Own your worth, create that alignment, and live a life that brings you both joy and fulfillment. *You* are the source of your happiness, and *you* have the power to design the life you desire.

VISION FOR THE FUTURE: YOUR GROWTH ROADMAP

As you embrace the information and BS exercises here in *Bullshift! Money Does Grow on Trees*, consider this your starting point, not the finish line. You've now built a foundation for a growth mindset and learned how to realign your thinking so your money tree can thrive. But what comes next? Your future success will depend on your ability to continue nurturing your money tree and applying the insights and lessons you've gained from the Bullshift Process.

Imagine your life one year from now. What do you want to see? How do you want to feel? Picture your business thriving, your stress reduced, and your mindset sharp and focused. These aren't just dreams, they're achievable outcomes if you stay committed to your growth. The work you've done so far has set the stage for long-term transformation, financially and personally, but your future depends on consistent actions and self-investment.

Start by creating a vision for your future. Take time to map out where you want to be financially, emotionally, and professionally. Write it down. Be specific. What will your daily life look like when you're operating at your fullest potential? Use that vision as a compass to guide your decisions and actions. And don't just stop at envisioning it! Work backwards from your goals to determine the smaller, actionable steps you need to take daily, weekly, and monthly to get there.

Along the way, don't forget to measure your growth. Just like you would track key metrics in your business, track your personal development. What beliefs have you shifted? How has your money mindset grown to support your business growth and other goals? Where have you gained confidence? What new opportunities are showing up in your life? Celebrate those wins, no matter how small, because they prove the process is working.

Your vision isn't a far-off dream; it's the roadmap to the life and business you've always wanted. It's the prosperity you've worked so hard to achieve. Stay connected to that vision! Use the Bullshift exercises, tools, and mindset shifts presented in this book as your guide. The more you practice, the more your reality will shift to reflect your highest aspirations.

Finally, remember that setbacks are part of the process. Growth isn't linear, and there will be times when old doubts creep back in, when results aren't as quick as you'd like them to be, or when you feel overwhelmed. That's okay! Revisit this book, go back to the Bullshift exercises, and refocus on your vision. Every challenge is an opportunity to strengthen your resolve and move closer to the life you deserve.

Your future is bright, abundant, and filled with opportunity. Continue investing in yourself, stay true to your vision, and trust that everything you need is already within you. This is just the beginning.

CONTINUE THE JOURNEY

Invest in yourself and your future! Contact me or find another coach who believes in you, even when your belief wavers (because it will). Surround yourself with a supportive community of people who understand the power of growth and who will cheer you on. Set strong intentions and remember to celebrate along the way. Put a little bit of vacation in every day to bring joy and relaxation into your routine. When you reach your next milestone, share your Bullshift success story with others who need to hear it. Your journey is an inspiration.

Whatever path you choose, remember this:

You are worthy. You are capable. And you have everything you need to achieve your dreams!

About the Author

Marla Tabaka is a business coach, author, and mindset expert who has spent more than twenty years helping entrepreneurs break free from self-doubt, scarcity thinking, and survival-mode decision making. Her work blends practical business insight with neuroscience-backed mindset tools to help people grow confident, profitable businesses without burning themselves out in the process.

Marla is an Inc.com contributor and has been featured in outlets including *Time Business* and *Thrive Global*. Through her private coaching, group programs, and workshops, she has worked with thousands of entrepreneurs across industries, helping them rewire limiting beliefs, strengthen emotional resilience, and step into leadership with clarity and confidence.

Known for her direct yet compassionate style, Marla doesn't teach hustle-for-hustle's-sake or surface-level positivity. Instead, she helps entrepreneurs understand how their brains are wired, why old patterns keep showing up, and how to create real, lasting change from the inside out. The Bullshift tools shared in this book have been tested, refined, and proven through years of real-world application with courageous business owners willing to do the inner work that drives outer success.

Marla believes that when mindset, strategy, and self-trust align, success stops feeling like a constant uphill battle and starts feeling sustainable, intentional, and deeply satisfying.

To learn more about Marla and her work, visit *marlatabaka.com*.

www.ingramcontent.com/pod-product-compliance
Lightning Source LLC
LaVergne TN
LVHW050537160826
845677LV00011B/2070

9798994281208